CASINO MARKETING:
THEORIES AND APPLICATIONS

PART OF THE
CASINO MANAGEMENT ESSENTIALS SERIES

Kathryn Hashimoto

East Carolina University

Prentice Hall

Boston   Columbus   Indianapolis   New York   San Francisco
Upper Saddle River   Amsterdam   Cape Town   Dubai   London
Madrid   Milan   Munich   Paris   Montreal   Toronto   Delhi   Mexico City
Sao Paulo   Sydney   Hong Kong   Seoul   Singapore   Taipei   Tokyo

To a very special person who has endured much during the production of this series of books. Thank you for your immense patience and loving support without which I would surely have not succeeded.

Library of Congress Cataloging-in-Publication Data

Hashimoto, Kathryn.
   Casino marketing : theories and applications/Kathryn Hashimoto.
      p. cm. —(Casino management essentials series)
   Includes index.
   ISBN-13: 978-0-13-199614-4
   ISBN-10: 0-13-199614-2
   1. Casinos–Marketing.   2. Casinos–Management.   I. Title.

HV6711.H38 2010
795.068'8—dc22

2009008653

Editor in Chief: Vernon Anthony
Acquisitions Editor: William Lawrensen
Development Editor: Sharon Hughes, O'Donnell & Associates, LLC
Editorial Assistant: Lara Dimmick
Director of Marketing: David Gesell
Marketing Manager: Leigh Ann Sims
Marketing Assistant: Les Roberts
Production Manager: Kathy Sleys
Project Manager: Kris Roach

Full Service Project Manager: Yasmeen Neelofar
Creative Director: Jayne Conte
Cover Designer: Margaret Kenselaar
Cover Art/image/photo[s]: Glowimages/ Getty Images, Inc.
Manager, Rights and Permissions: Zina Arabia
Manager, Visual Research: Beth Brenzel
Manager, Cover Visual Research & Permissions: Karen Sanatar
Image Permission Coordinator: Kathy Gavilanes

This book was set in 10/12 Palatino by GGS Higher Education Resources, A Division of Premedia Global, Inc. and was printed and bound by Courier Companies, Inc. The cover was printed by Courier Companies, Inc.

Pearson Education Ltd.
Pearson Education Singapore Pte. Ltd.
Pearson Education Canada, Ltd.
Pearson Education—Japan

Pearson Education Australia Pty. Limited
Pearson Education North Asia Ltd.
Pearson Educación de Mexico, S.A. de C.V.
Pearson Education Malaysia Pte. Ltd.

Prentice Hall
is an imprint of

www.pearsonhighered.com

10 9 8 7 6 5 4 3 2 1

ISBN-13: 978-0-13-199614-4
ISBN-10: 0-13-199614-2

BRIEF CONTENTS

CONTENTS

PREFACE

This book on casino marketing is an attempt to link the gaming industry to the business environment and its theoretical underpinnings. This book is different from its competitors in that it uses and discusses different marketing theories to teach fundamental knowledge before applying the information to the industry. Therefore, the readers accomplish two goals at one sitting. They learn about fundamental marketing practices as well casino industry applications. The gambling information in this book has been pulled from personal knowledge learned from 30 years of researching, teaching, and writing in the field; gambling practitioners; and industry trade journals.

Gambling is a business like any other in many ways, and yet different. One still needs to know about strategic planning, consumer and organizational buyers, segmentation, target marketing, and assessing the uncontrollable environment that surrounds and impacts the casino. However, no other industry has had such a checkered past—its historical precedents and its links to crime, addiction, and other unsavory characteristics. Therefore, it is vital for a manager to understand the past history to assess how to handle the present and future.

Chapter 1 is a traditional overview of the industry and the book. In order for Christopher to write Chapter 2 on strategy, he talked to nine different managers from many levels of responsibility in a variety of casinos to learn what the industry does for strategic planning. Then, he combined the theoretical knowledge of strategy to the practical experiential information to write the chapter. These two chapters are the major underpinnings for the rest of the book as we explore the uncontrollable environments (external factors) that dictate how casinos' product, price, place, and promotions should change.

Chapter 3 is similar to many marketing books in that it discusses the different uncontrollable variables (external factors) that impact any business. However, each one is evaluated in terms of how it specifically affects the casino industry. All of these macromarketing environments converge on consumers and organizational buyers as they decide at which casinos they will gamble and how they make those decisions. So, Chapters 4 and 5 explore general theories of purchasing behaviors and motivations along with how these theories apply to decisions on which casinos are favorite choices. Finally, Chapter 6, on market segmentation and positioning, explores how to divide the population into more manageable, similar groups and then how to position the casino product, price, and promotions to attract those audiences.

The last part of the book discusses the micromarketing or the controllable factors that use the information from the environmental scanning from the previous chapters to determine what decisions should be made to circumvent threats and take advantage of opportunities. Since the games are discussed in *Gaming Methods: Games, Probabilities, and Controls*, the first title of the series, we do not dwell on this aspect. We do evaluate the service-profit chain theory, which Gary Loveman helped popularize, to assess how to create a competitive advantage for the casino. Simply put, this theory says, "treat your employees with respect and they will be the cornerstone for your profitability." In the same vein, the casino pricing has also been discussed in the gaming methods book and the second book of the series, *Casino Financial Controls: Tracking the Flow of Money*. Therefore, we leave the details of pricing to these books and explore a relatively new pricing strategy that has revolutionized the industry: revenue management. The impressive decision software for RMS (revenue management system) take the difficult quantifiable decisions that assess the profitability of each player or group, calculates the scores, and then allows humans to take this information and do an intuitive final assessment.

As with other hospitality enterprises, once the casino is built, the location is set. Therefore, the question becomes how attractive is the setting and how are gamblers going to get there. Drawing people to the casino depends on how accessible the location is and how many different modes of transportation are available. It also helps to understand location and transportation issues so that one can decide what type of promotions to use. Finally, Chapter 11, the last chapter, ties the book together by summarizing the information in a holistic framework to show how it all fits.

This book is unique because it merges marketing theory and uses it as a jumping-off point to demonstrate how casino marketing decisions are made. This is not a marketing book with a few casino examples, but a synthesized casino marketing book.

ACKNOWLEDGMENTS

I appreciate all my friends in the industry who came to my aid with advice, information, and practical experience. Unfortunately, they cannot be cited in the book because some of the information was confidential. However, you know who you are and I thank you.

I also thank the reviewers for their insightful comments. They are Priscilla Bloomquist, Ph.D., New Mexico State University; Dan Creed, Normandale Community College; Donna Faria, Johnson & Wales; Evelyn K. Green, The University of Southern Mississippi; Paul Howe, Morrisville University; Jayne Pearson, Manchester Community College; Jack Tucci, Mississippi State University; and Jim Wortman, University of Houston.

To George, David, and Chris I thank you for writing some of the chapters with your special knowledge in the area.

Kathryn Hashimoto

CHAPTER 1

INTRODUCTION TO MARKETING

Kathryn Hashimoto

Learning Objectives

1. To learn of the long history of gambling
2. To understand the roles of social responsibility and ethics to gambling
3. To learn of the many issues concerning gambling prior to legalization
4. To learn the details of the historical factors affecting gambling
5. To learn the details of the external forces that affect gambling
6. To learn the details of the internal forces that affect gambling
7. To be familiar with what are considered the overall successes and shortcomings of gambling
8. To understand the importance of personnel issues to gambling
9. To understand the importance of the questions of government regulations and gambling addiction to the rise of gaming

Chapter Outline

Introduction
Social Responsibility and Ethics
Issues Before Legalization
Historical Factors
External Forces

Internal Forces
Successes and Shortcomings
Personnel
Other Questions
Conclusion

INTRODUCTION

To introduce casino marketing, we should start with some definitions. According to *Webster's* dictionary, *gambling* is defined as "to play or game for money; anything involving a like risk or uncertainty."[1] In this book, gambling discussions will be restricted to legal forms of gambling performed in a specially designated facility called a "casino" or "house." Therefore, lotteries, pari-mutuel, and sports books will be peripheral to, but not the central focus of discussion.

To begin, it is important to know a little bit about the infamous history of gambling. Gambling has existed ever since two people first sat together. After all, how do you think two cave dwellers decided who was going to throw the first rock at that night's expected dinner (that woolly mammoth over there)? Later, in Greek mythology, when a person wanted to make a difficult decision, he/she went to the oracle to ask for guidance. For example, if a maiden wanted to get married, she would go pray at the temple of Aphrodite (the goddess of love) for advice. The high priestess would also pray and ask for a sign. One or two dice would then be tossed and the gods would express their wishes through the number that came up. Usually, it was the rich and famous who went to the oracle. In Rome, gambling occurred more often at the mineral spas and baths where people soaked in the waters to be healed. Betting on cards and dice was convenient and helped to while the time away. In addition, the possibility of winning a bigger fortune by using one's skills and wits was exciting. So, in one location people could get physically well, increase their fortune, and improve their mental facilities by simply going to the baths. The rich, who did not have to work, were constantly looking for distractions from the boredom of their lives. Betting relieved that monotony. As a result, gambling developed as a pastime for the aristocracy. However, the church frowned on all the fun and frolic. Thus, historically, gambling has been considered to be one of life's major sins.

SOCIAL RESPONSIBILITY AND ETHICS

Gambling has had a difficult history. Aristocrats did not want peasants to gamble because peasant losses would deplete the taxable income that the rich needed to live. As a result, gambling was kept illegal. Another reason to keep the fun of gambling limited to the aristocracy was that it was considered a form of divine intervention. Aristocrats typically used a form of dice cast by priests to aid in difficult decisions such as going to war. Later, gambling was banned because winning money, not earning money through hard labor, was considered to be a sin by the church and sanctioned as evil, and as the devil's work or pastime. As lotteries crossed over into America, greedy lottery organizers were run out of town when they were corrupted by the massive wealth they could gain. Gambling was not only considered sinful, but it also created thieves . . . a clear indicator that gambling was evil. Then, when the Mafia took over the casinos in Las Vegas, gambling reached its pinnacle of social disgrace.

As a result of this history, social responsibility and ethics play a very important part in the casino industry today. With every new jurisdiction that considers legalizing gambling, the opposition cites social problems as a reason against the legislation. For example, gambling has been blamed for higher crime rates. According to conventional wisdom, when casinos come to town, crime rates increase. However, once the number of tourists is taken into account compared to the entire population, research suggests that crime rates increase for the first several years, but then drop below the pre-casino numbers. Similarly, the demise of local restaurants has also been cited as a reason not to allow casinos in a region. Folklore says that local restaurants that operate outside the casinos go out of business when casinos come to town. In fact, according to government data, the same pattern occurs as in crime rates: restaurant numbers diminish for a couple of years after the opening of casinos, but then the number of restaurants increases, the number of employees goes up, and wages increase. Other negative factors such as personal bankruptcies and suicides have been studied for links to gambling. However, there is not enough research on these topics, as the findings have been contradictory. There is also a very large research database on gambling addiction, which will not be explored here because of its size. With all of these negative or controversial perceptions about casinos and gaming, marketers must be alert for opportunities to create positive images and to educate the public on the differences between folklore and objective research findings when making decisions about gaming issues.

ISSUES BEFORE LEGALIZATION

Because of these claims, proprietary, regional, and state studies all extensively explore the various aspects of life in a community before and after gaming is legalized there. Theories such as tourism development cycles and social disruption theories have been used to evaluate quality of life issues before, after, and in projected trends of casinos. Tourism development cycle theories generally explain that the social "carrying capacity" of a region has an initial positive change that occurs during the early stages of development that reverts to a negative change as the community reaches its carrying capacity. On the other hand, **social disruption theory** believes that there is an initial negative change in quality of life that becomes positive as the community adapts to its new environment. Social disruption theory defines disruptive influences not only as just crime, bankruptcy, and addiction, but also as publicly visible nuisance crimes, the physical decay of communities, the presence of litter on streets, homelessness, and traffic congestion. There appear to be mixed findings in impact studies on these theories, depending on the community, type of disruptive influence, and whether the respondent is a gambler or not. Many states and regions have asked market researchers to develop these impact studies so that they can evaluate strategies on whether to allow casinos to operate, what circumstances should be created to control gambling and its impacts, and how residents feel about the casinos. As a result, it is critical to know what public perceptions are so that damage control and promotions can address these issues. For example, understanding that addiction has played a role in deregulations in gambling in the past, casinos are creating many programs in responsible gaming to allay the public's fears.

Because of these negative claims against gambling, casinos have higher taxes than other industries (from 5% to 70%), and pay special fees for additional police protection. For example, New Jersey casinos pay an additional Casino Reinvestment Development Authority (**CRDA**) tax of 1.25% to help rebuild Atlantic City. Harrah's Casino in New Orleans funds $2 million to help market the city and another $2 million for "social funds." In addition to taxes and special fees, casinos also fund, promote,

FIGURE 1.1   Tourists bring in outside money to a town.

and work with Gamblers Anonymous and other social programs. However, the negative image of casinos is difficult to change. More research needs to be conducted on target markets that might be influenced by the growing positive findings of objective research. Keep in mind that people tend to block information that is contrary to their current belief system. Because of their history and reputation, casinos work hard with various groups so that no one can say that they have shirked their social responsibility to the community.

As you can see, unlike most other industries, gambling, as a product, has had a very bad reputation. However, as economic hardships have befallen different geographic areas of America, politicians have recognized the immediate monetary advantages of casinos on taxes, employment, and regional development. Therefore, legalized gaming jurisdictions have multiplied as government budgets have been squeezed by their need for more money. The casinos have provided needed revenues for state and local governments and, as a result, governments have come to rely heavily on gaming revenues. During this process, attitudes have slowly changed and despite their controversial nature, the casinos of today are very popular. In America, for example, casinos have had three times more attendees than major league baseball games and five times more attendees than skiing and other sporting events.[2]

HISTORICAL FACTORS

As Americans discovered gaming was a recreational activity, 26% of the population over age 21 went to a casino, which amounted to over 310 million visits annually.[3] This meant a change in attitude. When the only gambling venue was Las Vegas, people had to plan their vacation deliberately to gamble. Once Atlantic City opened its doors with its bus programs, people could spend less time reaching a gambling destination—only a couple of hours, which is just a day trip. As a result of the bus tours that did all the driving for the customer, the densely populated Northeast corridor was introduced to legalized gambling. In the 1990s, Steve Wynn suggested that gambling was an alternative way to spend entertainment dollars. It was a form of recreation, like going to the movies or eating out. It was a short vacation from daily life, to have fun and relax and maybe walk away with more than the cost of dinner. As the popularity of casinos has grown, more than 80% of adults agree that going to a casino is an acceptable form of entertainment for themselves and others. If those numbers were broken down, 54% of Americans said that gambling was acceptable for anyone, while 26% said that while gambling was not for them, it was an acceptable form of entertainment for others. Only 4% of the American population believed that casinos were not acceptable for anyone.[4]

All of this historical information is important because developing a marketing plan is all about understanding the industry—the outside forces that impact the business and the internal decisions that are based on research and knowing your customers and your employees. Strategic planning begins with knowing who you (as a business) are and where you come from. Part of that assessment is comprehending the importance of the external environments (**macromarketing factors**) or things you, as a business, cannot control, but influence the way that you do business. This information is gathered through research and allows you to evaluate what type of consumers you want to attract to your casino. From there, you can decide what your strengths and weaknesses are as a product, and plan ways to enhance those strengths through detailed product, pricing, place, and promotions strategies.

FIGURE 1.2   Wynn Casino in Las Vegas.

EXTERNAL FORCES

To begin a discussion about marketing, one must understand the macroenvironments that surround a casino. Thus far, we have explored the history of gambling and how it has impacted the current uncontrollable environment. Understanding where you come from allows managers to explore the external forces that cannot be controlled by the industry, but have great impact on the way a casino does business. These forces are the political/legal environment, the economic environment, and the social/cultural environment.

Today, it is the political and legal environments that control the regulations and laws that govern what a casino can and cannot do. Legislators make decisions on employment laws for hiring and firing personnel. Legislators also mandate elements of a casino's design, square footage limits and usage, and the extent of allowable amenities. Ultimately, government makes the decision to allow gaming, and then controls the process.

Whenever the debate to legalize gambling appears, one of the positive effects of gambling that is usually cited is its improvement of the economic environment. Unemployment decreases as employment and jobs are created. More jobs mean more taxes to improve living conditions. As people spend their newly created wages, spin-off developments of banks, grocery stores, drug stores, and so forth, are needed to take care of the local residents.

On the other side of the debate on legalizing gambling is gambling's perceived effects on the social environment, such as a rise in crime, addiction, and underage gambling. These concerns have often brought gambling down. Can these perceived effects be controlled? Can the casinos create programs that will satisfy the public's desire to keep problems at a minimum? It is the people themselves who must decide whether gambling is an unethical, immoral activity, or an activity like any other. Gaming can be one of many recreational alternatives for a Friday night, or a possible vacation activity choice. However, people are heavily influenced by the rhetoric of legislation and the pressure of special interest groups.

The culture of the United States as it developed into a nation is reflected in the casino industry. There are several trends that started and then adapted to the changing present. Originally, in European culture, the rich were the ones who gambled. However, in the egalitarian new country of America, anyone, rich or poor could gamble. Wealthy plantation owners mingled with trappers and explorers on riverboats and in casinos. This trend generated a mass consumer movement to the casinos. Today, like America itself, with its big cars, large houses, and gigantic grocery stores, casinos have also become immense. However, in the beginning, the bars that housed the gambling tables were small, and their surveillance and management were simple—one man and one gun. As casinos grew in size, corporations were needed to run their operations. Management teams took over the one-man controls. Computers created a new way to make management decisions and control all the different operations.

When these external environments are good, the competitive environment increases, and more casinos enter the arena. Going back to our history lesson, during the 1980s, as state governments were looking for ways to increase their revenues, the regulatory environment lowered its resistance to casinos and allowed them into the jurisdiction. As other nongaming states saw the money pouring into the casino states, they too began to think about casinos as a positive economic tool. In addition, Native American tribes began to

FIGURE 1.3 Las Vegas Strip.

develop new casinos as the federal government created the Indian Gaming Regulatory Act (IGRA) to allow them to build gambling halls.

Ultimately, the people's buying behavior determines whether the casinos survive. The people make a decision to legislate for or against gambling. The consumers then gamble often enough and in great enough quantities, or not, to allow the casino to survive. As more casinos are allowed to operate and spread throughout the United States, the questions will be: Are there enough people to gamble in all the different types of gambling establishments? Will the competitive environment be unable to support all the casinos? How many casinos will survive when the dust settles?

Part of that answer will depend on who comes to the casinos. The casino marketers target certain groups of people to come to the casino. Special promotions are developed to attract the interests of those people. This also allows the casino to position itself in the minds of the public. Some casinos are considered small, friendly places for locals while other casinos are large, entertainment venues to attract tourists. For example, Bellagio and Wynn target an upscale market. Their products have luxurious suites, large elaborately decorated casinos, excellent, pricey restaurants, and well-trained employees. They charge more for their hotel rooms than most casinos and the table minimums are higher. However, they know the customers will be willing to pay these higher prices because they value the product and are looking for the status and prestige that using the services will provide. These casinos advertise in upscale magazines. On the other hand, casinos that cater to local clientele typically offer lower-denomination slot machines such as penny, nickel, and dime machines, and they offer a constantly changing entertainment venue to lure nearby residents to come to the casino for an evening's entertainment, often during the week. A relatively new market is the group business, especially meetings and conventions. Historically, only gamblers were considered suitable market segments. In recent years, as competition increased, marketers are building meetings and convention facilities to attract groups. Casinos target many different groups by offering them specific special promotions geared to their pocketbooks and their interests.

FIGURE 1.4 Gamblers laughing excitedly over a craps table.

Source: Bachmann, Bill/Photo Researchers, Inc.

INTERNAL FORCES

Once one understands the external forces that mold the casinos, one needs to examine what is happening inside the casinos. In this text, we will also look at the four internal forces that mold the casinos: product, pricing, place, and promotions. Most people consider the games to be the product of the casino. It is necessary to understand the casino product. How does the casino make money? How do the laws of probabilities affect the rules and profitability of the games? Because the product of casinos is money, more controls, including security and surveillance are needed to keep employees and patrons alike in check so that the casino can be run above board and clean. Since this series has a book devoted to the games (*Gaming Methods: Games, Probabilities, and Controls*), we will not explore this option. However, the newest trend in product development is the **service-profit chain**. This theory suggests that employees are the key to guest satisfaction. The employees create the image of the casino because they are the front line in guest contacts. As a result, if you treat your employees right and empower them to help guest problems, your guests will be happier. One study suggested that the cost of retaining a loyal customer has been assessed at 20% of the cost of attracting a new one. If you can increase 5% of customer retention rates, it yields a profit increase of 25%–125%. So, if your guests are happier, they will become more loyal to the casino, and profits go up.

Pricing in casino resorts is different from a traditional hotel or restaurant. Pricing can be considered when setting rules for the games as discussed in the games book and is also part of the accounting process described in the finance book of this series (*Casino Financial Controls: Tracking the Flow of Money*). Therefore, in this marketing book, we will discuss the newest pricing strategies. **Revenue management** is setting guidelines for increasing revenue at the casino and its amenities. For example, there are different objectives in filling casino hotels than traditional hotels, such as: What is the appropriate room price for a gambler? How does a casino price its product? Should we lower the price for walk-in business for that night, provided we have rooms available? Where do the familiar comps and credits fit in? Revenue management looks at all these different concepts to decide how to price its products to obtain the maximum profit.

Like most hospitality operations, a casino's location is set once the building is in place. Place limits or expands the options available for guests. In addition, some locations are more attractive to tourists, making it easier to draw people. On the other hand, like some Native American reservations, the casino is far away from the population density, and special promotions, tied closely to transportation, are needed to convince people to come. How do you get people from one place to another in the casino property? What channels (agents) do casinos and customers use when going to a casino? How do guests arrive at the casino? How easy or difficult is it to get to the location? Atlantic City was immediately successful because it sits within 2–6 driving hours from the densest population in the U.S. Las Vegas is an easy major highway drive from California and it has built a massive airport to cater to guests from around the world.

Finally, what is the message the casino wants to send? What promotions do they use? How do they create a synergistic effect in uniting all the different types of promotions so that customers do not get confused?

SUCCESSES AND SHORTCOMINGS

In 2006, Conrad analyzed marketing efforts in casinos.[5] He gave a list of things that casinos do well and not so well. See if you agree.

Things done well:

- Casino buffet
- Keeping track of the money
- Big name entertainment
- Service in hospitality areas
- Restroom cleanliness
- Gathering information
- Super Bowl events
- Following rules
- Giving away money in big promotions
- Security

On the other hand, Conrad says these are the things that are not done well:

- Slot service
- Welcoming new players to table games
- Coffee
- Employee recognition, the day-to-day "attaboys" and thanks for doing a great job
- Advertising—there's lots of it but not much is truly unique and hardly any of it is sales oriented or measurable
- Eliminating guest "waiting"—especially on weekends, there is still very little commitment to eliminating guest lines in numerous areas. Waiting guests weren't spending guests.
- Senior executives building relationships with customers
- Smoke-free environments—one of the casino customer's biggest complaints, "smoke-free" gaming remains largely an empty gesture in casinos

- Direct mail—casinos do a lot of it now, but it's still not extremely scientific or efficient
- Slot environments—rather than an appealing integration of sights, sounds, sensations, even smells, casinos are still at a "first generation" slot environment stage of general noise and smoke and discomfort
- First touch point welcomes—whether that first contact with casino guests is at valet parking, the player's club, the hotel front desk or a security station at the front entrance, our valued casino guests are more likely to be fee-processed than embraced

As you look through the good and bad items on the lists, you will notice that everything comes back to the customer's perceptions and their comfort. The characteristics that separate a service from a durable good can be classified as the four "I's" of service: intangibility, inseparability, inconsistency, and inventory. The fact that the product is intangible means that the consumer has a mental image of the product; but it cannot be substantiated by the five senses. In other words, it cannot be packaged and taken home. Inseparability and inconsistency refer to the fact that the product cannot be separated from the provider. The line personnel, not management, interact directly with the customer every time. Therefore, the experiences created by the dealer or waitstaff become the virtual reality of the casino experience. Inventory refers to the fact that once the visit has occurred, it is over. For example, you have 100 slot machines, but only 50 are played tonight. What happens to the other 50? Can you store those 50 and have 150 tomorrow? The "moment of truth" or the face-to-face encounter between employee and customers happen in an instant, but can leave a lasting impression. That is what we mean by the lack of inventory. Therefore, the experiences and perceptions created during each visit to the casino are the image of the product. The casino must create positive feelings on every visit. One bad experience can alter mental perceptions of the casino.

Therefore, these issues are what separate casino marketing from industrial marketing. However, as usual, the solutions are based on decisions about the product, price, place, and promotions. These are typical marketing issues. However, many casino marketing departments plan, coordinate, and implement special events for the sports like golf tournaments, boxing matches, and any special event that will attract large numbers of people and gamblers. In addition, because of the popularity of slots, they may focus on slot promotions.

PERSONNEL

The director of customer development is responsible for the overall marketing efforts to attract and keep players. For many casinos, developing and implementing programs to attract key casino players is a fundamental task, illustrated by the saying that 80% of a casino's revenue is generated by 20% of the players. Therefore, the director keeps track of the player rating reports, recommends comp status to the casino manager, and makes sure the casino hosts are giving invited guests first-class treatment. As part of this process, the director also oversees the credit application process, room reservation requests, and markers due and payable by invited guests.

Customer Development Representatives handle most of the clerical and logistical details such as contacting preapproved players, listing details for upcoming casino events, and coordinating all requests for room reservations. They also maintain computer reports on players, carry out telemarketing promotions, and act as greeters for VIPs either at the airport or at the casino. Finally, they work with casino hosts to help maintain top customer service standards.

FIGURE 1.5 Smiling employees create the perfect image for the guests.

Source: MGM Mirage.

VIP service representatives are often found at the front desk of a hotel/casino attending to the needs of casino VIPs upon arrival and initial check-in. Many casinos have a special VIP lounge adjacent to the front desk where the players can be registered, welcomed, and given a gift. Their job responsibilities are similar to front-desk concierges and their job is mainly to service invited casino guests to make them feel extremely pampered and welcomed.

Casino hosts are the key people who work to make high rollers have a good time. You could call them expediters since they act to make sure everything is in order. As a result, they solicit and book major players for the casino. Once the high rollers agree to come, the hosts handle their rooming accommodations and any special requests. They maintain contact with players while they are in-house and help handle the marker collections. Finally, they strive to create an ambience of casino entertainment for the high rollers and make sure that any problems that arise are handled instantly.

OTHER QUESTIONS

These questions concerning the external and internal forces affecting casinos are ones that everyone must ask if they are interested in the gaming environment. Casino gaming operators face other serious questions, both about their business and about the environment in which they operate. Should a new casino in Iowa be more of a destination area like Las Vegas or a day trip like Atlantic City? What kind of people should the casino attract? Should a casino hotel use the hotel as an amenity? Traditionally, hotel operations have been used to keep customers at the casino. Should the hotel or food service operate as a profit center in its own right? These decisions will alter the pricing strategy.

In examining the broader perspective, local government regulators are developing rules for casinos to protect the area's social environment, but should regulations be tough, like in Atlantic City, to prevent problems before they arise? Alternatively, should regulations be used to create a good environment for casinos to flourish, and allows for crack downs only when trouble occurs? Is the objective of gambling to promote tourism and generate income from people outside the town or state, or are casinos another business and entertainment center for townspeople? If the objective is tourism (i.e., drawing outsiders into town), what happens if every town has its own casino?

Casinos have also had to answer all kinds of social questions about the impact of gambling. Do casinos create gambling addicts? Does a person addicted to gambling have a personality that is prone to addictive behaviors? Is there something about the sport of gaming that creates the addiction? An interesting historical analysis suggests that Americans are still pioneers at heart. The frontiersmen were people who took risks and won. This kind of mentality is still respected in America. For example, a stockbroker is considered to have a good profession. However, is the rise of gambling fever Main Street's way of reflecting Wall Street's obsession with short-term speculation, instead of long-term investment? What is the difference between gambling in a casino and gambling on the stock market?

Conclusion

The chapters of this book bring you both sides of gambling issues to provoke thought. The organization of this book is based on a strategic environmental scanning of gambling. It begins with external factors that influence the way gambling develops, such as the economy, and the social, cultural, legal, political, and technological environments. Each of these factors is explored to show how they influence and structure casinos. Once it is understood how the outside world alters casinos, it is possible to look at the product, price, place, and promotions to show how these internal factors have developed and how management decision making has adapted to the outside pressures. Chapter 11 summarizes how marketing efforts affect the casino and its surrounding environment. When you finish this book, you should be able to look at an issue, think about the implications from the macromarketing environment, and then decide possible alternatives using the micromarketing options available to you.

Key Words

Social disruption theory *3*

CRDA *3*

Macromarketing factors *5*

Service-profit chain *8*

Revenue management *8*

Customer Development Representatives *10*

Review Questions

1. Discuss the nature of the long history of gambling.
2. Explain the roles of social responsibility and ethics to gambling.
3. Detail the many issues concerning gambling prior to legalization.
4. Discuss the details of the historical factors affecting gambling.
5. Discuss the details of the external forces that affect gambling.

6. Discuss the details of the internal forces that affect gambling.
7. Discuss the factors that are considered to be the overall successes and shortcomings of gambling.
8. Detail the importance of personnel issues to gambling.

9. Discuss the importance of the questions of government regulations and gambling addiction to the rise of gaming.

Endnotes

1. Webster's New University Unabridged Dictionary. (1979). New York:Simon & Schuster.
2. Nealon, J. T. (2006). Take Me Out to the Slot Machines: Reflections on Gambling and Contemporary American Culture. *South Atlantic Quarterly, 105*(2), 465–474.
3. Harrah's Survey 04: Profile of the American Casino Gambler. Harrah's Entertainment.
4. AGA State of the States 2005: The AGA Survey of Casino Entertainment, www.americangaming.org
5. Conrad, D. (2006). Things Done Well—and Not So Well. *Casino Journal, 19*(1), 25.

CHAPTER 2

STRATEGIC PLANNING

CHRISTOPHER M. HURLEY

Learning Objectives

1. To understand the role of marketing in strategic planning
2. To understand the necessity of planning in the casino industry
3. To learn of the proper length of time for the planning process in different situations
4. To learn the importance of corporate strategic planning
5. To be familiar with items to be taken into consideration in strategic planning
6. To understand the importance of goal formulation in strategic planning
7. To be familiar with the importance of strategy formulation in planning
8. To be familiar with the methods of implementation of a strategic plan
9. To understand the importance of feedback and control to strategic planning

Chapter Outline

INTRODUCTION

This chapter will detail the process of a strategic plan as part of a casino property and the role of marketing in it. The chapter will discuss why planning is so important to the successes of any business, as well as the typical time frame that is considered when devising a plan. The chapter explains the common information that is taken into consideration by casino properties and the implementation processes that companies follow. To ensure success within the business world, feedback from customers and employees is needed to control the plan that is currently being implemented. The general business policies of the casino industry are focused on all aspects of the strategic planning process.

Much of this chapter was derived from in-depth interviews of strategic planners from casinos at many levels. However; because of the confidentiality of the information, we have agreed not to cite specific people or properties who have offered their insights to make this chapter unique; we thank them for their knowledge (Figure 2.1).

THE ROLE OF MARKETING IN STRATEGIC PLANNING

Strategic planning can be a simple process. Fundamentally, it involves three major steps: focusing, forecasting, and formulating. *Focusing* refers to the ability to assess the current state of the business. Where has it been? What external or uncontrollable factors will affect its current status? And, where is the company at? On a personal level, when you are looking for a job, a company will ask for your resume to "focus" on where you have been and what you are currently doing. A common marketing tool to help you assess the current

FIGURE 2.1 People with Light Bulb Thought.

state of affairs is called a **SWOT analysis**. This stands for Strengths, Weaknesses, Opportunities, and Threats. A SWOT analysis is an important step in planning and its value is often underestimated despite the simplicity of its creation. The role of the SWOT analysis is to take information from the environmental analysis and separate it into internal issues (strengths and weaknesses) and external issues (opportunities and threats). Once this is completed, the SWOT analysis determines if the information indicates something that will assist the firm in accomplishing its objectives (a strength or opportunity), or if it indicates an obstacle that must be overcome or minimized to achieve desired results (weakness or threat).[1]

The strengths and weaknesses assess the product. What are the good points and problems that the product has? For example, a strength might be that you have job experience. A weakness could be that you do not have a degree. Weaknesses should be noted so that you can decide how to turn them into strengths. For example, in this case you could decide to get a degree. In addition to evaluating the product, you also need to analyze the uncontrollable environment around you—opportunities and threats. This analysis is also called *environmental scanning*. For example, after 9/11, people were afraid to board airplanes. This is something that could not be controlled, but it did affect business around America. As a result, casinos tried to attract people who could drive to the casino as opposed to flying.

The second step is to forecast. Given the current state of affairs, where should the company be in a year, ten years or whatever time frame you choose? Again, on a personal level, you are studying this book because you want to improve yourself for some project or job sometime in the future. That is forecasting or setting objectives to reach some goal.

The third step is the most important and the most complicated. How do you get from where you are now to the set goal? This is the plan. First you need to look at your projected goal and break it down into smaller objectives. For example, in order to get into a school, you may need to

1. decide you want to continue your education,
2. decide where you want to go to school,
3. search out the different schools and ask for applications,
4. receive applications and fill them out,
5. ask for letters of recommendations,
6. send the applications back, and
7. send your letter of acceptance when you are admitted.

Each of these objectives entails specific actions. They are also sequential in time so you have to succeed at the first objective before moving on to the second. Setting a time for each objective to be finished is called **time management**. In this way you know that when you meet each objective, you are closer to achieving the overall goal. When you have completed step 7, your goals are reached in the time you set. All along the path, there must always be time to check progress. How is the plan working? Have things changed? Do you need to reassess the goals and objectives? Some people think that strategic planning is a waste of time because things always change, so what is the point? However, we need direction. We might plan a driving vacation from New York City to New Orleans in May. As we drive, we find that there is a nice town where we want to spend more time. We can change our plans, but still our goal is to reach New Orleans. If we did not have our goals and objectives set before we started, we would be driving aimlessly around with no place to go.

Strategic management is an approach that focuses on positioning the organization for success—both now and in the future. This concept integrates planning, implementation, and assessment and incorporates concepts from strategic planning, operational planning, quality improvement, and institutional effectiveness. Strategic management is indeed a process for business organizations to use in forming a strategic vision, setting casino objectives, crafting casino strategy, and executing that strategy. Over time, as the environment changes, management can adapt and initiate whatever corrective adjustments are in their vision, objectives, strategy, and execution as deemed appropriate. A satisfactory strategic plan must be realistic and attainable so as to allow managers to think strategically and act operationally.[2]

In a business setting, many aspects of a strategic plan heavily revolve around the marketing portion of the process. The goal of business is to generate profits. As long as private capital invests or loans the money for the construction and operation of a casino, profit is the driving force of the project. To achieve these profit goals, business applies a multidisciplinary approach including human resources, accounting/finance, operations, and marketing. The objective of marketing is to create demand for the business by utilizing two primary approaches: product marketing and program marketing. The goal of **product marketing** is to stimulate demand by conceptualizing and delivering a good or service that meets or exceeds a consumer need, want, or expectation at a price that creates a real or perceived value. The goal of **program marketing** is to stimulate and channel that demand among consumers who might not buy the product unaided (i.e., for product reasons alone) by using various marketing techniques, like promotions and incentives. An effective marketing effort must plan for both efforts. It is difficult to develop successful program marketing efforts around products that are substandard or misaligned with the marketplace. Likewise, it is difficult to develop successful product lines without effective advertising, promotions, and loyalty programs.[3]

NECESSITY OF PLANNING

It is not a surprise that one of the most important aspects of running a successful business is the planning that is put into it. A planning process helps with thinking rationally about a long-term perspective and being able to figure out where the business is headed in more of a strategic, rather than reactive, fashion. It is hard for a company to measure whether or not it is successful unless it has a plan in place to measure the market and the potential changes within the market. You can't know whether you have attained your goals if you don't set them. If you do not have any benchmarks, how will you know if you are going in the right direction?

Gaming is a highly capital-intensive industry where strategic planning serves as the driver. It is used not only to maximize revenues and resources for a company, but also to pull everything into focus so that a much broader view can be seen of the overall intended direction. When constructing a plan, it is important to understand where the market currently is, what it is going to take to maximize that market, and implementing a long-term plan on how to achieve that goal.

LENGTH OF TIME FOR PLANNING PROCESS

It is likely that the more planning is done, the more efficient and effective the results will be. With that in mind, it is also important that no plan is set in stone, so things can be altered according to unforeseeable futures. Although data analysis can give a rough estimate of what is going to happen in future markets, ultimately markets are an uncertainty that can only be tentatively planned for. According to experts who have spent extensive time within the gaming industry, it is common for a company to take a minimum of at least five years into consideration when creating a strategic plan. For larger companies, it is common to have a 10–20-year strategic plan on the horizon as a very visionary perspective. It would then be adjusted down to a five-year plan with more specifically directed details. Ultimately, as the company narrows its focus, a one-year plan with extremely specific approaches is used to assess what and exactly when things need to be done. Each individual property has at least one yearly planning meeting to discuss what steps need to be taken. That plan is then presented to a divisional or corporate level where alterations can be made if necessary.

Often, monthly meetings are held within properties as a means of continuing communication. People who are involved in these meetings typically include the heads of each of the departments such as the Rooms, Hotel Operations, Casino Operations, Food and Beverage, and Property Management departments. Since each area of a property is intertwined within another, it is important that there be an open line of communication from one to the next (Figure 2.2).

FIGURE 2.2 Keeping the lines of communication open is very important for strategic planning.

CORPORATE STRATEGIC PLANNING

A corporate strategic plan identifies the organization's priorities and sets the broad framework within which departments and individuals with the organization will work. The strategic plan links directly to the corporate mission and vision, and becomes the tool the organization uses as a compass every day while it takes positive strides toward achieving its vision. "Everything in a company grows out of its mission statement—its behavior, its structure, and all of its strategic planning and decisions. A **mission statement** sets the tone for the whole company and provides it with focus. It lays out what the company stands for and gives family members and nonfamily employees alike something to live up to."[4]

THINGS TAKEN INTO CONSIDERATION

One of the first aspects that are taken into consideration in a planning process is taking a look at the current revenue stream. How much money does the company actually have to work with? Where should that money be targeted to best help the company? For example, it would not make sense for a gaming corporation to launch a mass marketing campaign across the country when it only has three properties all located in the West. In order to ensure that funds are directed in the right place toward the right customers, it is important for companies to have a substantial amount of data relating to the surrounding environment.

After speaking with several executives in the casino industry, it was unanimous that a large portion of what is taken into account when forecasting a plan revolves heavily around data analysis. This consists of analysis such as financial projections, competitive analysis charts, growth projections, and trend analysis. These are used to appropriately forecast what is going to happen to the marketplace in the future. Since what is going to happen one year from now is always an uncertainty regardless of ten years down the road, historical factors are taken into consideration. The current economic conditions throughout the country are factors that have the ability to have tremendous impact on the gaming industry. If people fear that the country is slipping into a recession, they might be a little more hesitant about spending their disposable income on gaming entertainment. It is a common trend that each company usually collects these types of data sets themselves or from another corporate entity rather than outsourcing.

Along with data sets comes a process of **risk assessment**. This entails companies targeting security risks that might prevent them from achieving their goals. These types of risks can come in the form of current competitors in the market, emerging competitors, or the economy's market as a whole. In the gaming industry, it is important to keep in mind that social issues as well as changing legislation could affect a property. Once these types of risks are targeted, a company will weigh out the likelihood of their occurrence and what potential impact they might have on the company. For a company to identify these types of risks and handle them accordingly means that no surprises (or at least none within reason) should catch them off guard.

A company's competition is always considered when making any type of strategic plan. It is essential to understand what the competitors are currently doing, along with what they have historically done within a more recent time frame and what effect their actions have had on the business. In an ever-evolving industry, companies need to stay ahead of the game as much as possible. If the direct competition to a business has devised a better way of doing something, whether it is a new product line or a faster way to serve, the competing company must alter its plan accordingly to best fit the situation.

Companies seek out and analyze business trends and customer behavior in order to counteract various trends. Types of customers are usually divided up by location segments and revenue segments to determine how much each customer might be worth. It is imperative to know whether those segments are growing or shrinking, and where the customers are coming from to fully capture the opportunities to grow those segments. A company's personnel are also a factor that comes into play when making a plan. There must be people within the company who have both the capabilities as well as the desire to strive toward common strategic company goals. Having measurable and achievable goals is a good start for each employee to be moving in the same direction. Companies can also further outline a plan that is less specific and distant to employees. That is why it is vital that there be short-term goals that are within reach for employees to pursue.

The current location of a business, both demographically as well as within the industry, must be considered to decide which is the best path to take. Today the legislation and policies for the casino gaming industry differ vastly from state to state. As a result, it is important to target market the appropriate sector as well as to realize that what might work in one state might not necessarily work in the next.

GOAL FORMULATION

The strategic planning approach has been reflected in large parts of the strategy literature as a rather centralized process. The CEO serves as the key strategy maker who conceives the strategic plan, and imposes its implementation on the rest of the organization. In this framework, top management sets long-term goals and medium-term objectives. Rational analysis of the firm's competitive position guides the formulation of appropriate strategies in view of the firm's goals and objectives, and strategic choices are enacted through the organization's operational policies. Hence, the corporate strategy process is typically described as a hierarchical process where top management outlines an overall strategic plan based on corporate goals before general managers develop their goals and strategic business plans and middle managers set functional goals and strategies. Subsequently, strategic control systems assess how the organization proceeds toward established strategic goals and objectives (Figure 2.3).[5]

FIGURE 2.3 Forecasting a target is very important for a strategic plan.

STRATEGY FORMULATION

Strategy formulation is a leadership skill as well as a process that leaders use to focus their companies on where they need to adapt to their customer needs to better prepare their employees. Strategy formulation is vital to the well-being of a company or organization. There are two major types of strategy: (1) corporate strategy, in which companies decide which line or lines of business to engage in and (2) business or competitive strategy, which sets the framework for achieving success in a particular business. While business strategy often receives more attention than corporate strategy, both forms of strategy involve planning, industry/market analysis, goal setting, commitment of resources, and monitoring. The formulation of a sound strategy facilitates a number of actions and desired results that would be otherwise difficult. A strategic plan, when communicated to all members of an organization, provides employees with a clear vision of what the purposes and objectives of the firm are. The formulation of strategy forces organizations to examine the prospect of change in the foreseeable future and to prepare for change rather than to wait passively until market forces compel it. Strategy formulation allows the firm to plan its capital budgeting. Companies have limited funds to invest and must allocate capital funds where they will be most effective and derive the highest returns on their investments.[6]

IMPLEMENTATION OF A STRATEGIC PLAN

A strategy is of course only as good as its implementation. A company may have an impressive strategy for conquering the market, but if it fails to take the right steps, the strategy is meaningless. The means of implementing strategies are called **tactics**. The tactical execution, while crucial to the success of any strategy, is not a traditional part of the formulation of that strategy. However, many companies have been successful in discovering successful tactics and building their strategies about "what works." The implementation experience, whether favorable or unfavorable, also directly informs the strategy revision process or any new strategies, as the company will take into account its successes and failures when choosing future paths.[7] After speaking with several people within the gaming industry, it was commonly mentioned that there are three main components when a company is implementing a strategic plan: commitment, credibility, and communication. In order for a plan to work, there must be commitment to that plan starting from the top down. The best way to assess change in accordance to the plan is to see that subordinates themselves change in the same direction. If everyone on board is fully committed to the same goals and headed on the same path, it is much more likely for a plan to succeed. These types of goal settings must be recognized company-wide and established in a way that each department can contribute to them.

First, key business strategies are focused on capital expenditure studies, marketing projections, financial trends, labor summaries, and all strategic marketing initiatives. This type of information has to be set forth in terms of financial data so that it can turn into the basis for a company's financial plan. Based on the financial plan, a company can accurately set the targets necessary for each department to attain.

Second, the plan that is being made by the company has to be feasible. In most cases it is feasible, but it is not that uncommon for a beginning-of-the-year plan to drastically exceed financial projections within a year's time. This is one of the reasons for the inclusion of so many different people in the planning process, to make sure all information used is accurate and credible when determining the appropriate path.

Third, in order for any plan in any type of organization to work seamlessly, there has to be an open line of communication between the departments themselves as well as to and from the corporate office. The easiest and quickest way to foresee an upcoming problem or fix one that has already occurred is through immediate discussion of what is happening. This is one of the reasons why feedback from an implemented plan is so important to the company. Employee and customer feedback can enhance the way that a plan is altered or originated the next time around.

Finally, one of the most important things to consider when devising a plan is not only the intended revenue, but also the customer and employee satisfaction that the plan is going to provide. One of the best ways to make sure that a plan is going to withstand the test of time is to make sure employees are satisfied with their environment and the intended direction of these goals. According to one executive, it is common for a company to align incentive compensation with the goals of the company. Doing that not only helps the company to attain its goals, but it also motivates the employees from a financial standpoint and also aids in their satisfaction.

Plans are typically worked out at the corporate level with heavy input from the actual properties themselves. Each property will have a team that consists of the president and general manager along with a few other people from their senior staff who share their ideas as to what direction the company should move in. These people typically include heads of departments such as Marketing, Food and Beverage, Casino Operations, Human Resources, Finance, and Customer Service, each of whom focuses on the customer experience. Each operating unit within the property builds toward the general plan and focuses in on what needs to be executed in their departments to help achieve the overall plan.

FEEDBACK AND CONTROL

Companies need to keep track of their own progress on the key goals and objectives outlined in the strategic plan. The company must be objective and flexible enough to realize whether the strategy is no longer appropriate as it was first conceived, and whether it needs revision or replacement. In other cases, the strategy itself may be fine, but the communication of the strategy to employees has been inadequate or the specific steps to implementation haven't worked out as planned. This evaluation and feedback of the strategy formulation provides the foundation for successful future strategy formulation.

During the process of implementing the strategic plan, the company may come upon a period where things might not be going the exact way they had hoped, and benchmarks previously set are not being hit. Performance of a company is usually monitored on a monthly basis and it is not hard to recognize when a plan has fallen off track. When this type of situation happens, the plan needs to be reevaluated and altered accordingly. For example, it is not uncommon for a company to create a plan with the misconception that their growth rate might be higher than it actually is. If this were to occur, the plan must be reanalyzed around a more realistic growth forecast and implemented not only for the short term, but for the long term as well. These types of decisions need to come from the top and work their way down to the various departments of a property.

There is a financial plan that is put into place that specifies exactly how much each department needs to contribute to that plan as well as the marketing tactics that are going to allow the company to achieve those results. This is followed by an operating review that is commonly conducted monthly to analyze how the company performed both as a whole and departmentally toward that plan. If it is a widespread trend throughout each of the departments that all are not hitting anticipated numbers, then the overall company plan might need to be altered from the top. On a smaller scale, if only one department is showing unfavorable results while the others might be exceeding expectations, it is clear that only that department needs to be reanalyzed.

The key to maintaining a healthy plan is to modify problems immediately when things start to go wrong. It is much easier to fix a problem that has been going on for a week rather than three months. If it is a small matter that needs to be altered for better outcomes, then the process should not be too extensive. On the other hand, if a company is faced with a series of reoccurring problems such as not meeting benchmarks, high turnover rates, or high customer dissatisfaction, then a much broader approach needs to be taken to fix the problems.

Conclusion

While it is certain that the need for planning in a casino is inevitable, the process and steps that are taken differ vastly. Whether the approach taken by a company is a more short term rather than a 20-year plan comes down to the specifications and goals that a company has in mind. It is important for companies to focus on how much of an asset employees are to them and what an important role they play in achieving desired goals. If a plan is put in place properly, implemented correctly, and adjusted accordingly, in time, success and desired results should be certain. Then again, in an uncertain market a plan might sound easier to achieve on paper than in the real world.

Key Words

SWOT analysis *000*

Time management *000*

Strategic management *000*

Product marketing *000*

Program marketing *000*

Mission statement *000*

Risk assessment *000*

Tactics *000*

Review Questions

1. Explain the role of marketing in strategic planning.
2. Detail the necessity of planning in the casino industry.
3. Discuss the proper length of time for the planning process in different situations.
4. Detail the importance of corporate strategic planning.
5. Detail the items to be taken into consideration in strategic planning.
6. Explain the importance of goal formulation in strategic planning.
7. Explain the importance of strategy formulation in planning.
8. Detail the methods of implementation of a strategic plan.
9. Explain the importance of feedback and control to strategic planning.

Endnotes

1. Ferrell, O., Hartline, M., Lucas, G., Luck, D. (1998) *Marketing Strategy*. Orlando, FL: Dryden Press.
2. Mudd, R. (2005, October). Developing a Strategic Management Plan, *Indian Gaming, 39*.
3. Macomber, D. (2001). Preparing a Marketing Plan. Retrieved April 2008, from *Urbino.net*.
4. Nelton, S. (1990, November). The Mission of finding a Mission—Defining Business Mission Statements. *Nations Business*. Retrieved on April 28, 2008, from http://findarticles.com/p/articles/mi_m1154/is_n11_v78/ai_9089666
5. Porter, M. E (1980) *Competitive Strategy*. New York, NY: Free Press; Richards, M. D. (1986) *Setting Strategic Goals and Objectives*. St, Paul, MN: West Publishing.
6. Strategy Formulation (2006) *Encyclopedia of Business*. 2006. Business Reference. Retrieved on April 28, 2008 from http://www.referenceforbusiness.com/encyclopedia/Str-The/Strategy-Formulation.html.
7. Ibid.

PART ONE

Macromarketing

External Factors that Impact on Doing Business

EXTERNAL ENVIRONMENTS

KATHRYN HASHIMOTO

Learning Objectives

1. To learn of the results of the 9/11 attacks on the tourism economy
2. To understand the effects of the historical environment on the gaming industry
3. To understand the effects of the natural environment on the gaming industry
4. To understand the effects of the mass media environment on the gaming industry
5. To understand the effects of the technology environment on the gaming industry
6. To understand the effects of the cultural/social environment on the gaming industry
7. To understand the effects of the political/legal environment on the gaming industry
8. To understand the effects of the economic environment on the gaming industry

Chapter Outline

INTRODUCTION

As we explored the strategic planning in marketing (Chapter 2), the first step was to assess the **macroenvironment** or external forces that surround a casino. This **environmental scanning** was part of the SWOT matrix to evaluate where we are now. These uncontrollable opportunities and threats encircle the casino and the analysis of these forces should be used to make decisions on the things, such as product, price, place and promotions, we can control.

THE RESULTS OF 9/11 ON THE TOURISM ECONOMY

For example, the events of 9/11 were uncontrollable and altered the way that people thought. This historical cultural catastrophe for Americans made consumers, especially those with children, rethink their plans to fly and to go to crowded places such as Disney World and Las Vegas. As a result, this changed the social environment, especially for recreation, hospitality, and tourism. The political/legal environment closed ranks and tightened security and increased the legal rules governing air flights and travel. As a result of this one event, Las Vegas needed to rethink its future. Strategists said that people would not fly; therefore, casinos needed to focus on drawing limited visitors who could drive from a smaller geographic area. While other tourism destinations look for international visitors, Las Vegas was more impacted because the high rollers from Asia thought the risks were too high to come to Las Vegas. Therefore, planners expected lower visitor rates in the hotels, restaurants, and tourist destinations. For the first time in its history, Las Vegas had massive layoffs as the casinos prepared for the economic disaster by decreasing the number of employees, which in turn meant lower profits and taxes. As a result, this major terrorist event resulted in businesses faltering as fewer consumers traveled. Fewer consumers meant fewer jobs, which resulted in people fearing for their job security, and thereby curtailing their vacations, recreation, eating out, and buying. This created a downward economic spiral as consumer fear of spending escalated, which resulted in less travel, and decreased the number of jobs available.

During this same time, New Orleans planners had a different vision and environmental scanning analysis. Fall is convention season. It is very difficult to cancel meetings and conventions because it is hard to notify everyone. As a result, many groups continued their plans to arrive in New Orleans, which meant that more tourists made the trip. As you can imagine, people who had to fly reconsidered attending, but drive-in traffic came. In addition, the spring time was tourist season with Mardi Gras, French Quarter Fest, and JazzFest, to name a few of the major events. It was hoped that the four-to-five-month breathing space would allow consumers to reevaluate their fears and that they would begin to travel again. Because of this more optimistic forecast, the **microenvironment**, or things we can control also differed. Businesses that relied on tourism did not layoff as many people. They tried to keep their employees by reducing hours for everyone. The Convention and Visitors Bureau created a promotional campaign titled "Be a Tourist in Your Own Town." The campaign aimed to draw locals to go out to dinner more often to save restaurants from failing. In addition, locals were lured to tourist attractions to see why outsiders came to their town. Because of this different focus on the forecast for the next year, the product, price, place, and promotions also changed to meet the different predictions. So, depending on how strategists analyze the macroenvironment, different outcomes and decisions are made in the microenvironment.

FIGURE 3.1   Jazzfest was one of the big events that brought back tourists to New Orleans.

This chapter will explore seven of the external forces that cannot be controlled by a casino, but have great impact on the way the casino does business. These forces are historical; natural, mass media, technological, cultural/social, political/legal, and economic.

THE HISTORICAL ENVIRONMENT

The culture of the United States as it developed into a nation is reflected in the casino industry. There are a couple of trends that started in the past and adapted to the changing present. Originally, in European cultures, the rich were the ones who gambled. However, as the pioneers came to America and spread throughout the land, people were free and equal to bet. However, more men than women took the opportunity to gamble since most gambling took place in saloons where women of questionable reputation were more likely to frequent. However, when slots first entered the market in San Francisco, it was generally believed that they were to attract the ladies. Men gambled at the tables, but their female companions became bored and dragged the men away from their gambling. Slot machines were seen as a way to entertain the ladies since those machines were perceived as mind-less frivolity. As a result, gambling in America was a mass consumer trend. This trend led to casinos targeting a wide general audience of all people, which was unique to this continent. Today, like the vast space of America itself, consumer products in general reflect this size in cars, houses, and casinos.

Throughout the history of gambling, there has been a consistent cycle of legalization. It begins when governments need money. As a result, they look at gambling as a quick fix to their problem and they legalize it. People like to gamble and gambling's popularity increases. However, social problems arise in the form of addiction, crime, and juvenile gambling. As these problems increase, the social outcry forces governments to deregulate gambling.

Understanding this cycle, casino managers have assessed the problems and directed a new course of action. These new thinkers believe that the past does not have to predict the future. Responsible gaming is the wave of the future. Casino management is stepping up to the plate and assessing ways it can help. With alternatives and solutions, gambling can have an extended life cycle.

THE NATURAL ENVIRONMENT

The **natural environment** consists of the natural resources required by marketers or affected by marketing activities. Anyone involved in tourism is responsible for protecting the environment and ensuring sustainability. More and more in hospitality, people are beginning to understand that protecting the natural environment will assure that the human race will be around in the future. As opposed to polluting the environment in which we live, hospitality is working to create a more "green" environment. You see it in hotels when they ask you to keep your towels and sheets for a little longer so that there is less water and detergents used. Instead of chopping down the trees when constructing a building, planners are preserving the surrounding land. However, the discussion to protect the environment also includes casino developments in New Orleans and Mississippi that have had a tremendous negative impact on the ecosystems along the Gulf. As a result, casino managements are looking to find new paths to save the ecosystems and control their impact on the environment.

As casino managers become aware of a casino's impact on the natural environment, other places are also joining the green movement. For example, the state of California made a compact with the North Folk Rancheria of Mono Indians to create a new casino in an unincorporated area of Madera County rather than in the tribe's Sierra foothills Rancheria. This mutual agreement changed the location to off-sovereign land so that the tribal land of the Sierra National Forest and the Sierra Vista Scenic Byway could be preserved.

Another example of ecological awareness is the St. Regis Mohawk Tribe's Akwesasne Mohawk Casino working with Clarkson University to develop methods to reuse kitchen waste. For example, the casino uses 3,000 gallons of vegetable oil every month in its restaurants. The oil will be converted into biodiesel fuel and used to run the tribe's maintenance vehicles, thereby recycling the oil and using less fossil fuel. These are just a few new ways that casinos are exploring and coming up with creative solutions to protect the environment.

THE MASS MEDIA ENVIRONMENT

In the traditional microenvironment, promotions is one of the ways that corporations get their message out to their consumers. We talk about controlling the process; however, there is another side of the **mass media environment** that is part of the macroenvironment. When the news media are going after a headline story, businesses cannot control the slant of the story or even the story itself. When the press headlines a story titled "Mary Smith Wins a Million Dollar Jackpot at XYZ Casino," we are thrilled. It doesn't cost the casino any money and gamblers flock to the casino to emulate Mary Smith's good fortune. On the other hand, the press also goes after stories that we may not like, as illustrated by a headline like "Casinos Create 100,000 Addicts a Year in the State."

Sometimes the media slants a story to suit their position. For example, there are two possible wordings for this story: "100,000 addicts" or "around 2% of the population" in the state are at risk to become problem gamblers. The statistics are similar but one creates a negative spin while the other is less sensational, but also accurate. As a result, it is important for management to understand what perception the local press has about gambling. If the media are negative toward casinos, it is important to work with them to create a more positive atmosphere. This is an example of understanding the macroenvironment. Decisions can be made to turn a threat into an opportunity.

THE TECHNOLOGY ENVIRONMENT

The **technological environment** in the world is rapidly changing, and as a result, industry must constantly upgrade to obtain the maximum benefit. The casino world is seen as incorporating the latest in technology while the hospitality industry has been described a slower to upgrade. Casinos use technology in all of their departments from surveillance to restaurants to hotels to table games to slots. Surveillance uses technology to track criminals or cheats. In fact, when a specific casino is stumped on a cheat, it calls on a global security/surveillance company that taps into the casino surveillance system, watches the cheat in action, describes what is happening, and formulates a plan. With satellite technology, the global surveillance person does not even have to be in the same city to help. Restaurants use computerized order systems that automatically send a guest's order to the kitchen, notifies the wait staff when the food is ready, scans the credit card for payment, and even prints out a receipt when finished. Hotels use PMS (property management systems) for housekeeping to notify the front desk when a room is ready and then to track the room when the guest arrives. PMS also notify the front desk guest's preferences, problems the guest has had in the past and their history, and then housekeeping when the guest checks out.

FIGURE 3.2 Club cards allow guests to keep track of their comps.

On the casino floor, technology also plays a key role. The most important development has been putting player's club card slots in the tables and slot machines so that all
guests, with all their information, can be tracked. Also, coinless machines have been a great
advancement, at least from the casino's viewpoint. Casinos don't have to worry about how
much the coins weigh and where they are located in riverboats. After all, the coins are so
heavy that if not placed correctly they could capsize the riverboat, especially when the
waves are large. Checking the number of coins in a machine so that jackpots can be paid out
is always a difficult venture. Keeping track of all those coins is a time-consuming task. Now
any transactions are instantly recorded at the machine and on the mainframe, with players
knowing exactly how much credit they have and what their current comp rate is. This
decreases the amount of work with coins, thereby saving the casino labor costs.

CULTURAL/SOCIAL ENVIRONMENTS

Do you know what the difference is between the **cultural and the social environments**?
The cultural environment includes institutions and other forces that affect society's basic
values, perceptions, preferences, and behaviors. A culture is a long-term set of values and
beliefs that a group of people have in common. For example, Americans believe that individual efforts make a difference, so we look to people like Steve Wynn or Gary Loveman to
set the path for innovative ideas on casino trends. On the other hand, the social environment is our day-to-day living and activities. What types of recreation do you do? How do
you spend your time off from work? Gambling is relatively new to the public's perception
as a recreation venue and a fun addition to the social environment in a region or town.

Betting and gambling have always been a part of American history, but it is not usually discussed in the history books. Gambling was always a form of recreation, from the
pioneers to the plantation owners. However, in America the levels of the social acceptance
of gambling have run in a cyclical pattern. Some might say that we can never get rid of
gambling because it is in our blood. Who would be crazy enough to give up everything
they knew to try their luck in an untamed wilderness? Only a gambler! Therefore, some
have theorized that America was settled by people with a betting spirit.

On the other side of the debate on legalizing gambling is gambling's perceived
effects on the social environment, such as a rise in crime, addiction, and underage gambling. These concerns have often brought gambling down. Can these perceived effects be
controlled? Can the casinos create programs that will satisfy the public's desire to keep
problems at a minimum? It is the people themselves who must decide whether gambling
is an unethical, immoral activity, or an activity like any other. In this view, gaming can be one
of many recreational alternatives for a Friday night, and a possible vacation destination.

Unfortunately, some people want to get more than their fair share of gambling
money, and crime rates increase. Some also cannot control their desire for more and more
excitement, and they wager their entire fortunes on the turn of a card or a throw of the
dice. In the past, addiction and suicide rates increased as broken men wagered the family
estate and women sold their bodies to pay for their gambling debts. In Monaco in the
1700s, there were actually postcards depicting different forms of suicide. As the negative
impacts of gambling grew, the social outcry became louder and louder, until finally public
pressure became so great that the government mandated that gambling stop.

However, this is a pessimistic view. Does it have to be like this? Is man destined to
relive old behaviors, or can we learn from history and change the traditional patterns?

As the gambling industry evaluates its future, it has worked with governments and other organizations to prevent the cycle from reoccurring. Casinos have funded many different projects to find solutions to these issues. The 2002 survey by the American Gaming Association (AGA) revealed that Americans have noticed the efforts of the commercial casino industry to promote responsible gaming. Nearly two-thirds of Americans have said that they think the gaming industry is doing a good job of eliminating illegal and underage gambling, compared with much lower approval levels for other industries dealing with illegal or underage use of their products.[1]

POLITICAL/LEGAL ENVIRONMENTS

The political environment is made up of laws, government agencies, and special interest groups that influence and limit the activities of various organizations and individuals in society. When Nevada first approved gambling, there were no role models, so it was more of a laissez-faire mentality. It was assumed that the industry would be fine and additional regulations could be approved later on. As we know now, the Mob came in and dominated the casino industry. It took years for the legitimate casino owners to oust the Mob from their holdings. As a result, when Atlantic City approved gambling, the distrust of gambling combined with the Mob connections required that strict legislation and regulations were the order of the day. As a result, new departments and regulatory agencies were created to dictate security policies for every aspect of the casino, from approving owners and managers to licensing casino employees to even mandating how many hours of training dealers must have before working.

When riverboats and Native American casinos joined the industry, each jurisdiction had to decide which model was best for them and then modify it. The riverboats not only had to pay attention to the gaming commissions and the state police, but because they were operated on water, they also had to comply with the Coast Guard and other water commissions! As you have learned from the other books in this series, the Native American tribes are regulated by the federal government, so they face not only a compact with the state but also maneuver with all the federal agencies as well. The **political/legal environment** is no picnic for casino operators, but they must know all the rules and regulations in order to comply or get shut down. Of course, the ultimate concern is that the casinos can be deregulated and closed down by the state and federal governments.

ECONOMIC ENVIRONMENT

The **economic environment** consists of factors that affect consumer purchasing power and spending patterns. As one studies casino development, many questions arise. Casinos are purported to improve the economic condition of the communities who host them. For example, the Native Americans who build casinos quite often then have money for better homes, hospitals, and schools. In Tunica, Mississippi, where casinos were legalized in 1990, everyone who wants to work, can. There are more than enough jobs to go around, and the pay level is high. On the other hand, skeptics point to Atlantic City and say that things have not changed in that town. However, since 1978, the casinos there have given a percentage of their revenues to the city for redevelopment to improve city conditions. Should the casinos be required to fund forms of urban renewal such as this? Is this fair? Are other businesses required to do the same? Is it the casinos' problem that social conditions have not changed?

FIGURE 3.3   Casinos bring back jobs.

Source: Michael Newman/PhotoEdit Inc.

Whenever the debate to legalize gambling appears, one of the positive effects of gambling that is usually cited is its improvement of the economic environment. Unemployment decreases as employment and jobs are created. More jobs mean more taxes to improve living conditions. As people spend their newly created wages, spin-off developments of banks, grocery stores, drug stores, and so on are needed to take care of the local residents. Because gambling brings in cash quickly with little time lag, it is a very appealing revenue source. Also, residents become upset when taxes are raised, whereas they do not in general have the same concerns with gambling taxes. Whenever the federal and state governments spend more money than brought in with taxes, they contemplate legalizing gambling. When casinos are developed, jobs are available, taxes are paid, and people spend money. Lifestyles for the residents improve. In addition, the infrastructure of the town is paid for by these taxes, and so life is good.

Beginning especially in 1976, the rationale for legalized gambling exemplified a return to the classic theme. Governments in the 1990s were strapped for cash. Some towns had even gone bankrupt, an unheard of concept before the 1980s. Even today, as the population ages, more people are retiring every year, with fewer young people to support the system. Therefore, social programs need more money to operate. Also, in terms of "real" income, people have less disposable income than in previous generations, and the desire to gamble is still very much alive. State lotteries are a classic example of people being willing to spend money to gamble and not complain, even though at least 50% of the revenues from the lotteries are kept by the state. America is in the midst of gambling fever, and its social acceptance is on the rise.

Perhaps this change in attitude partially resulted from the positive economic impact that communities received from the casinos. In 2008, more than $5.8 billion was received by state and local governments in direct gaming taxes, which was an 11.3% increase over 2006.[2] This is a nice sum, considering that before casinos, most of these areas were struggling to survive. For example, along the Mississippi River, manufacturing companies had

FIGURE 3.4 Uncle Sam smiles and stands with his hand out expectantly for all the new taxes he receives from casinos.

Source: Images.com.

left for foreign countries to look for cheaper labor and taxes, leaving gaping holes in the economic development of many states. Young people were also leaving the region to seek employment. Many people do not realize that casinos pay taxes and fees far in excess of other industries.

ENVIRONMENTAL SCANNING

All of these macroenvironmental forces impact businesses in isolation but also in combination. Depending on how positive the outlook for the casino business, more casinos might decide to open, creating a highly competitive location. On the other hand, competition might decrease as the market becomes saturated. To be successful, a casino must assess gamblers' needs and wants, and provide a better utility than its competitors. Therefore, casinos need to keep track of three variables when analyzing its competition in terms of its share of (1) market, (2) the consumer's logical mind, and (3) the consumer's loyalty or heart.

In addition, these macro forces also impact the consumers. Because of the history of casinos, consumers are concerned about the casinos' integrity and the honesty of their games. Depending on the local mass media coverage of casinos, the local population can be influenced for or against the desirability to have a casino in the area and whether they want to gamble. This impacts on the politician's desire to support or argue against gaming laws and controls. Part of this assessment of the casino environment is the question of how the public perceives gambling.

As a result, consumer research has explored both the perceptions about gaming as well as the perceptions about gaming's impact. One of the consistent results from this research is that the more people gamble and spend time at a casino, the more positive their perceptions are of the impact of casinos on local life. Another constant finding is that perceptions of gambling can be subdivided by religious affiliations. Catholics tend to have a more positive attitude toward gambling than Protestants, which is reflected in studies on participation in gambling activities and the level or frequency of gambling. On the other hand, sects like Southern Baptists, Mormons, Jehovah's Witnesses, and Muslims tend to discourage gambling and casinos.

This type of information is important to marketers as they assess whether to have gambling in a region and also to evaluate what kind of marketing should be used and where advertising should be placed in the various media. In addition, perceptions about gaming change as people are more or less in tune with their church. Perceptions are difficult to assess and more difficult to change. Even when presented with objective data, people tend to maintain their beliefs. We will explore this subject more in Chapters 4 on consumer markets, Chapter 5 on meetings and conventions, and Chapter 6 on market segmentation. Understanding buyer behaviors is at the heart of marketing. One definition for marketing is: find a need and fill it. Therefore, marketing is all about what people want. Then, once this knowledge is acquired, you can develop or create a product that will satisfy that need and want in consumers who have money.

Conclusion

Responding to the environment is an important planning strategy. Many companies feel that the marketing environment is uncontrollable, and therefore one should not waste time trying to plan for something that is so variable. However, keep in mind that you can't define success by reaching your goals, if you don't have any. So begin by defining the environmental areas that you believe require monitoring, such as the political/legal environments. Determine how that information should be gathered. Who should gather it? What materials should be obtained, and how often should this process be done? Implement the data collection plan. Decide who should analyze the data and report it. How often should the planning bodies meet to assess this information and what it means for business? Then, create a strategic plan to circumvent the threats or take advantage of the opportunities presented by the macroenvironmental forces. This allows you to carefully plan ahead for the future rather than managing by crisis and making decisions to bandage problems for the short term. In other words, take a proactive rather than a reactive approach.

Key Words

Macroenvironment *28*
Environmental scanning *28*
Microenvironment *28*
Natural environment *30*

Mass media environment *30*
Technological environment *31*
Cultural/social environment *32*

Political/legal environment *33*
Economic environment *33*

Review Questions

1. Discuss the results of the 9/11 attacks on the tourism economy.
2. Describe the effects of the historical environment on the gaming industry.
3. Describe the effects of the natural environment on the gaming industry.
4. Detail the effects of the mass media environment on the gaming industry.
5. Detail the effects of the historical environment on the gaming industry.
6. Explain the effects of the technology environment on the gaming industry.
7. Explain the effects of the cultural/social environment on the gaming industry.
8. Discuss the effects of the political/legal environment on the gaming industry.
9. Discuss the effects of the economic environment on the gaming industry.

Endnotes

1. AGA State of the States (2008). The AGA Survey of Casino Entertainment. Retrieved June 15, 2008, from www.americangaming.org.

2. Ibid.

CHAPTER 4

CONSUMER MARKETS

KATHRYN HASHIMOTO

Learning Objectives

1. To provide an overview of the study of consumer behavior in order to help the reader understand how people make purchase decisions[1]

2. To explore the external and internal influences that persuade consumers to look for products and services

3. To understand the four stages of consumer decision making

4. To provide an overview of the five subdisciplines that the majority of consumer behavior research in the casino gambling field has been based on

5. To explore player demographics in order to gain insight into who the casino customer is

Chapter Outline

INTRODUCTION

I knew a retired couple who were very frugal. They were careful with every penny they spent. I could always find them at home, unless they were grocery shopping on Wednesday, or if Ruth was getting her hair done on Friday. One day, their daughter asked them to go on a bus to Atlantic City for the day. Although they were not sure they wanted to go, they agreed because it was an anniversary present from their children. They each received $20 in tokens and a free lunch buffet at the casino, and the bus had free food and drink during the trip. Wally sat on the boardwalk and ate his free lunch. So, Wally gained $20 because he didn't gamble. Ruth lost the $20 at the slot machines, but she was able to spend the day with her daughter. It was a pleasant day for all. Ruth's birthday was a few months later. Again the daughter invited them to go to Atlantic City, and this time they agreed more readily. Wally played his $20 because it was after all, "found money," and hit for $500.

Five years later, Wally and Ruth drive the three hours to Atlantic City because the bus doesn't give them enough time at the casino. They eat on the way in, because they don't want to waste precious gambling time once they arrive. On average, they go once a month and take $1,000 each. The money comes from presents for special occasions, their winnings, and Wally's extra work now that he is retired. Why do they go? They say it is exciting, a change from their daily routine, and it gives them a topic of conversation. In addition, Ruth shows everyone the picture that the casino took when she won $1,500.

What aspects of this story concern consumer behavior? All of them. **Consumer behavior** is the study of how, why, who, what, and where people make purchase decisions. It begins on a broad scale by exploring the external influences that persuade someone to look for a place to game or the products and services inside the casino, and then studies how these ideas are internally processed. From this stage, we look over the consumer decision process, which examines how people make their final decision to buy. In our story, the external influence was Ruth's daughter, who decided to buy the tickets. Wally and Ruth thought about what they had learned about casinos and gambling over the years and tried to reconcile these external ideas with their own values and norms. While their thoughts about wasting money at a casino were more negative, it was overpowered by their love for their daughter and the anniversary gift. Each of these steps is part of the buyer behaviors.

THE "HOW" OF CONSUMER BEHAVIOR: CONSUMER BEHAVIOR THEORY

Psychological Core: External and Internal Inputs

The study of consumer behavior begins with external forces, such as culture, social environment, economy, laws, and so on that a person cannot control. For example, some religions frown on any type of gambling activities.[2] For some, this relates to the puritan work ethic where work is everything, and if you don't work for something, it can't be good. Therefore, pleasure for its own sake is to be distrusted. This especially applies to gambling.

In American culture, norms and values have slowly changed over time from seeing gambling as an evil, immoral activity to gambling as recreation. Therefore, more people have included going to a casino as part of their social lives, which has been made possible because the legal and political environments have changed the laws to adapt to new economic and social conditions. For example, in one community when casinos were first proposed, 58% of community leaders were positive in general about the impacts of casino; 18%, ambivalent; and 24%, negative. However, when asked how casinos have lived up to their expectations, 58% said the impact was better than expected, 31% remained unchanged, and 9% thought the impact was worse than their original projections. As you can see, all of these various external forces impact a person's internal attitudes and values. The psychological makeup of an individual filters the external information and blends it with his/her personality.

The Process of Decision Making

There are four stages of the consumer decision-making process: problem recognition, information search, decision making, and postpurchase evaluation. For casino consumers, this process might begin by a friend wanting company when he/she goes to the casino. The invitation might spark a search for further information on the Internet, from a travel agent, or from another information source. This would be followed by the decision whether to purchase the casino product, and from where (i.e., direct purchase from the casino, travel agent, e-commerce, etc.). Once the person makes the decision, there is a post-purchase evaluation called *cognitive dissonance* where the person asks himself/herself whether it was the right decision. The information search phase would include conducting further searching for information on the product prior to the actual purchase or experience, and/or evaluating the purchase after the actual casino product has been experienced (the post-casino trip). The cognitive dissonance is a crucial stage for casinos. How consumers evaluate their experience after they return home (or the after-decision evaluation) will determine whether the patron returns. This is the stage when the person makes a judgment about the experience and whether it was worth the time and money. At this time, it is crucial for a casino to reassure the patrons that they had fun and they should come back. One of the ways this can be done is by sending an email or letter telling the gambler what a great decision is/was to come to the casino and offering an incentive for a return visit.

Whenever people go out for fun, they must agree on the decision, whether it is to go to a casino or to the movies or to dinner. A couple will discuss what movies are playing and whether they want to go see them; whether they want to go out with friends or by themselves to celebrate an occasion; or go to a casino for some excitement. For our example, let us assume that they decide to visit a casino. On the way home after the casino visit, the couple talk about how much they won or lost, and whether they should have left earlier or later. This entire scenario is the consumer decision-making process. The problem recognition stage was when the couple first thought about going out; the information search stage began as they pondered where to go; during the decision-making stage, they actually made the decision; and the postpurchase evaluation stage occurred during their discussion as they were coming back home.

As with any service, the client's experience and satisfaction is an individual thing. The virtual reality of the casino is in the mind of the patron. It is important to remember that this virtual reality can be easily altered by a bad experience or an unpleasant dealer. Understanding the consumer decision process helps the marketer to decide where to intervene in the process. For example, an advertising campaign should ideally generate excitement and anticipation that the casino is the only activity choice and there is no need for an information search. Therefore, gamblers will go from problem recognition straight through to purchase without any of the steps in between. This is the best possible scenario because it means that casinos have brand-loyal customers.

FIGURE 4.1 Knowing how people make their recreation decisions can aid casino marketers in creating messages to draw people to the casino.

THE "WHY" OF CONSUMER BEHAVIOR: PERSPECTIVES ON GAMBLING MOTIVATION

Man has always had a gambling streak. Down through the ages, every culture and every social stratum have played games of chance. There is something about the luck of the draw or the throw of the dice that attracts the risk-taking urge. People are drawn to gamble; after all, a common saying is "Ya wanna bet?" Why do we use that saying in all different types of situations? It has been theorized that since life was a big gamble, primitive man found a fascination with gambling as divination and primitive justice. To some degree, it made life a little less of a risk. Unpredictable events could be made predictable by throwing a die. This control issue is a powerful motivation for many people.

It has only been since the early 1900s that theorists have tried to answer the question of why people gamble. More people have become interested in gambling behavior as Americans embrace the idea of casinos. Consumers in 2007 spent less on commercial casinos than they did on home remodeling, quick-service meals, cable television, and soft drinks, but more than they did on movie tickets, candy, or computer and video game software.[3] In fact, consumers spent more than 34.13 billion in 2007, a 5.3% increase over 2006 totals and a 73% increase over the figure from a decade ago.[4] To understand why people gamble, the fields of economics, sociology, psychoanalytic theory, psychology, and the interdisciplinary nature of work and play have come up with their own ideas.

Economics

Economists believe that people are rational beings. Humans evaluate *all* the alternatives before making a decision. Therefore, one theory about gambling behavior is that people do not know the probabilities of winning. After all, rational persons would not deliberately make the choice to gamble knowing that they were likely to lose. However, this is too simplistic an explanation, and it doesn't explain the reality that there are many people who know the odds and still bet.

A possible explanation can be found in Veblen's theory of conspicuous consumption. Historically, gambling was a sign of wealth; therefore members of affluent classes gambled to demonstrate their social standing ("I am rich enough to lose all this money"). Another theory revolves around the personality traits of the gambler. People who avoid risk would not gamble; however if they did, they would underestimate the true probabilities of a loss and overestimate the chance to win. For example, "I have my lucky shirt on today, so I'm sure to hit big." Milton Friedman developed the **"utility of wealth theory."** He said that rational people will gamble if they place a high enough value on the chance of achieving wealth. In other words, a person realizes the true probabilities, but he/she wants the rewards so much that he/she will risk losing. Lotteries are an example of this theory. As you can see, many economists have tried to explain the draw that people have to betting.

Sociology

It is not surprising that sociologists would study gambling because it is concerned with the social rules and processes that bind and separate people not only as individuals, but as members of organizations. Gambling was perceived as deviant and gamblers were misguided, but they were not outcasts from society. Therefore, people who were frustrated and rebellious could blow off steam since gambling was perceived as an evil activity, yet still function as normal persons in society. Therefore, gambling acts as a safety valve for societal tensions.

In 1951, Bloch claimed that gambling was a retreat from the routine boredom of modern industrial life.[5] It was fun to break the rules and take a chance. It was an opportunity to take on a different role in life, and a great release from the social sanctions so that it was easier to go back to routine daily existence. Additional theories suggested that game participants receive temporary satisfaction unavailable in their everyday work environments; people who were not successful at their jobs could be winners at cards. Erving Goffman called gambling a surrogate for risk taking.[6] After working as a dealer in Reno, he suggested that gamblers could show courage, integrity, composure, and other character strengths that could not be demonstrated on the job or in normal life. Because we admire people who take risks and win, it proves one's superiority and mastery over life. To challenge and overcome an obstacle is a true test of one's strength, skill, endurance, or ingenuity.

Felicia Campbell devised a theory related to people in nursing homes.[7] She believed that gambling can be a positive part of normal human behavior. So, she advocated the placement of slot machines in nursing homes to improve the patients' quality of life. Gambling would provide stimulation to the patients in their days at the nursing home. Playing the slots would get people excited and increase adrenaline. As a result, blood flow would increase, which would help circulation. In addition to the health benefits, the nursing home residents would have a reason to get up in the morning and they would have fun during their day. It would also give them a common ground for talking with their friends and families thereby enhancing their social lives. As you can imagine, these suggestions were met with a great deal of controversy.

Psychoanalytic Theory

Psychoanalytic theory, a general term for a psychiatric model, can be applied to the study of gambling. The first known psychoanalytic study of gambling was conducted by H. Von Hattingberg in 1914.[8] After studying one addicted gambling patient, he concluded that the patient suffered from a generalized psychosexual inadequacy. In other words, problem gamblers had not successfully matured past their adolescent stage, and they substituted gambling for sex. Freud agreed with this diagnosis and added that gambling was a self-punishment that stemmed from the Oedipus complex. This is a developmental stage in a young boy's life when he has to choose a sexual role model. During this time, he wants to eliminate his father, so that he can be the sole person in his mother's life. For young boys who never matured beyond the Oedipal stage, this conflict leads them to lose everything at the casino in order to punish themselves for their bad thoughts. To enhance this thought, Robert LaForgue argued that gamblers found pleasure in the pain of losing and that psychic masochism was the reason people gambled.[9] Winning was also thus symbolic for forgiveness.

Psychology

Psychology (from the ancient Greek: *psyche* meaning *soul* and *logos* meaning *word*) is the study of behavior, mind, and thought. Two of the simplest gambling motivation theories are that (1) life is boring and the excitement of the game confirms that one is alive, and (2) people want to win money. The first theory would explain Wally and Ruth's experiences from the opening paragraphs of this chapter. The second theory is straight greed, to which we all can relate. Both of these theories are based on universal needs, which may explain why there isn't a demographic profile or combination of personality characteristics that can isolate potential gamblers.

Applying general psychological theories to gambling offers a series of gambling motives. Attribution theory suggests that people attribute their success to themselves, their skill, or their luck. For example, a gambler is on a winning streak or his/her luck is hot tonight. The losses are blamed on something else. Losses occur because the dealer is crooked, their companion has bad karma, the moon is in the wrong phase, or any other reason that comes to mind. Because losses are not a player's fault, it is easy to forget them or write them off as a fluke. It has been suggested that men tend to use this type of attribution more than women. Research indicates that women are more likely to explain winning on outside factors: "my good fairy was with me," or "the slot machine was ready to hit and I happened by." On the other hand, losing tends to be attributed to a personal failure: "I picked the wrong machine," or "I have a bad luck streak running today." This kind of thinking may explain why men's perceptions of winning are higher than women's perceptions. Both views tend to be inflated. This attribution of wins and losses allows people to believe that they have some kind of control over their fate. Also, younger gamblers have more of a feeling of control, which is why they tend to have greater win perceptions than older players. If you listen to people talk about their gambling experiences, everyone talks about the big win they had. Nobody talks about how much they played and lost before they won the pot. This little game we play in our minds keeps us feeling like tomorrow is another day to win. A feeling of control is important to gamblers.

Behaviorists believe that these mental games are normal, but it is really what people do and how they behave that is important. Given a particular stimulus, people are programmed to respond in the same way each time. This response pattern is based on the person's previous reinforcement to a stimulus. Sam puts a coin in a slot machine,

FIGURE 4.2   Many Elvis fans are drawn to these slot banks because they want to hear him sing. As a result, they will drop the maximum coins in the slot for the privilege.

and he is rewarded with a "hit." This sets up a pattern of behavior. When Skinner developed a **variable schedule of reinforcement**, which means that rewards were given at totally random times, the reaction of the animals to this stimulus-response cycle was predictable. The birds rapidly hit a key without slowing down until they were rewarded. Then they immediately began the cycle again because they were never sure when the next reward would be given. If you have ever watched people play at two or three slot machines at a time, you may notice a resemblance to Skinner's experiments.

Interdisciplinary Study of Play and Leisure

Interdisciplinary study integrates concepts across different disciplines. The casino gaming industry is a complex and multifaceted interdisciplinary field. Understanding the needs, wants, and motivations of both casino patrons and nonpatrons is essential for the continued growth and success of this industry. Today, thanks to Steve Wynn, visiting a casino or riverboat is perceived as play and leisure. Understanding the leisure preferences of casino patrons can enable the industry to position itself as a viable alternative to other competing forms of leisure activities.

What makes a person pick a casino destination versus Disneyland? When competing with other vacation spots, casinos can be successful based on affordable rooms and inexpensive good food. Many locations have great entertainment both on stage and off. Places like Las Vegas have every type of tourist attraction a person could want: art museums, amusement parks, theater, cultural events, and shopping. In addition, players take a shot at changing their lives when they sit down at a table or a slot machine. Gambling is the only recreation where a person could literally walk away in a different economic position in life.

THE "WHO" OF CONSUMER BEHAVIOR: PLAYER DEMOGRAPHICS

As we said earlier, there isn't a single demographic or psychographic profile that casinos can say "this is who gambles." All kinds of people from all walks of life and all socioeconomic levels gamble. However, we can discuss some generalities about gamblers. More than 25% American adults (about 26% of those 21 and older) made 320 million casino visits in 2006.[10]

- The median household income of U.S. casino gamblers ($53,204) is 16% higher than that of nongamblers ($45,781).
- Americans in upper-income brackets have the highest casino gambling participation rates and those in the lower-income brackets have the lowest casino participation rates. Nearly a third (32%) of individuals with household incomes of more than $95,000 gambled in a casino in 2003, while only 20% of those with annual incomes of less than $35,000 gambled in a casino.
- More than three-quarters of casino players own their homes, compared to 71% of nongamblers.
- The typical casino player is about the same age as the typical American: The median age of casino gamblers is 48 versus 46 for the adult U.S. population.
- The age bracket with the highest casino participation rate is the "empty nest" years of 51 to 65 (29%).
- Casino players are more likely than the national average to hold white-collar jobs: 44% versus 41%.

From these demographics, it would appear that there is a relationship between income and financial security and the amount of visits and spending of players. In addition, these statistics have remained fairly stable over the years.

Types

Today, there are three broad types of gamblers: compulsive, occupational, and recreational. One to two percent of people are **compulsive gamblers**. They may also live by gambling; however, they more likely live *for* gambling, continuing to gamble obsessively even as losses mount. For these bettors, gambling is not a rational process, and typically they may steal to support their habit, create family crises, and have high job insecurity. On the other hand, **occupational gamblers** believe that their skills will enable them to make money by gambling. They use a rational process with special bank accounts for gambling and file tax returns with the IRS (Internal Revenue Service) on their winnings. They spend a great deal of time learning probabilities of games and attend workshops that give mathematical calculations on the newest games. Some professional gamblers are indeed able to live off their winnings; however, this is obviously not a low-stress, sustainable employment strategy for most individuals.

For the most part, most people are **recreational gamblers** who view gambling as a leisure time pursuit. They can be anywhere from "high rollers" (large spenders on gambling activities) to "low rollers" (minimal spenders). This segment regards the gambling experience as another form of recreation within their individual lifestyle. Gambling activities will rank as just one of a possible bundle of other recreational activities such as shopping, sports, hobbies, and so on. Obviously, this is the largest group (around 98%), the majority of the people who enter a casino.

Casino marketers need to adopt different strategies, channels, and messages for these three segment types of gamblers. Casino patrons who are occupational or compulsive gamblers already have a vested interest in the casino industry. Contrary to some, casinos do not

FIGURE 4.3 Multiethnic group of people playing craps and gambling at blackjack tables at Players Casino, Lake Charles, Louisiana.

Source: Jeff Greenberg/PhotoEdit Inc.

make their money by getting people drunk or addicted. It is not good for business. Typically, casinos work with family and friends by barring compulsive gamblers from the property. They also have created responsible gambling programs and work with different groups to get help for these individuals.

On the other hand, recreational gamblers generally do not have a strong loyalty to casino gambling as an activity. To this segment, casino gaming is just one of many recreational opportunity options available to them. When making the decision to go gambling, this segment would typically weigh the costs and benefits of the casino experience with other forms of recreation. For example, a golfer might be hard to get off the golf course in his spare time but luckily he can't play in the dark. The marketing emphasis here is comparing the uniqueness of the casino experience to other recreation. Recreational gamblers also offer casino marketers the greatest future potential of market expansion, compared to occupational or compulsive gamblers, who usually require less marketing stimulation than recreational gamblers.

Lifestyle—Psychographics

Psychographics describe a consumer's personality, lifestyle, values, and attitudes. Differences in psychographics will, in turn, influence buyer behavior through such variables as the product and service benefits sought, product usage rate, brand loyalty, and readiness to buy. A common myth is that gamblers tend to be independent, financially unstable, and of a lower social class. However, studies like Harrah's annual report[11] repeatedly have dispelled long-standing myths about gamblers' lifestyles, socioeconomic status, and level of community involvement.

Casino gamblers tend to be more connected to community groups: particularly volunteer, fraternal, union, and political groups, while nongamblers are more active in religious groups. With very few exceptions, casino gamblers have greater confidence than nongamblers in government; business; and other institutions such as the military, financial institutions, local law enforcement, public schools, organized labor, and the criminal justice system. Casino gamblers are also politically active. Surveys have revealed that gamblers are more likely than nongamblers to have contributed money to a political candidate or cause (26% vs. 19%) and to have signed a petition in support of a political candidate or cause (51% vs. 42%) in the past four years. Casino gamblers utilize a variety of financial investment products, are relatively comfortable with their financial standing, and have a greater inclination toward saving and investment than the overall population. For example, gamblers are more likely than nongamblers to have a variety of investments, including savings accounts, life insurance, retirement/pension plans, mutual funds, stocks, real estate, money market accounts, bonds, and annuities. Gamblers are more likely to be comfortable with their financial standing as they age, whereas nongamblers are more likely to worry they will not have adequate funds for retirement. When making financial and investment decisions, gamblers are more inclined than nongamblers to seek expert advice and reference a broad array of resources. If presented with a large sum of money, gamblers are more likely to save or invest it, while nongamblers are more inclined to use the money to pay off debt.

Perhaps because of the financial security and involvement in the world around them, two out of three casino gamblers take at least one long vacation trip per year, while less than half of nongamblers do. Casino gamblers like to travel in style and are more likely than nongamblers to book upscale accommodations when they vacation. These data from Harrah's consumer questionnaires would suggest that people who go to a casino are politically and socially involved and financially sound. Because they have the discretionary money to satisfy their wants and needs, they gamble as part of their recreational lifestyle.

THE "WHAT" OF CONSUMER BEHAVIOR: GAMES

All kinds of people from all walks of life and all socioeconomic levels gamble. However, the reason people play different games tends to be more predictable. According to a study by Lowenhar and Boykin,[12] slots play is exciting and people drop coins to have a good time. It is probably not surprising to know that slot/video poker machines are the most popular game among both men and women, with 66% of male and 81% of female gamblers reporting they play electronic gaming machines most often. On the other hand, men, more than women, prefer table games by a margin of more than two-to-one (20% vs. 8%), with blackjack/21 the single most popular table game. Younger adults are most likely to play table games, with 18% of 21- to 35-year-olds reporting that they play table games most often. However, many people play keno to pass the time while waiting for a meal or something else to happen.

FIGURE 4.4 Exterior of Harrah's Casino and Hotel in Atlantic City, New Jersey.

Source: Rudi Von Briel/ PhotoEdit Inc.

THE "WHERE" OF CONSUMER BEHAVIOR IN CASINO MANAGEMENT: PLACES

Not surprisingly, the top two U.S. casino markets in revenue for 2007 were Las Vegas and Atlantic City. However, Chicagoland, Illinois, was third, followed by Connecticut, and Detroit.[13] Additionally, the top seven casino markets had total gross gaming revenues exceeding $1 billion and were located in different regions of the United States. The market that experienced the largest increase over 2006 totals was Biloxi, Mississippi, which saw its gross gaming revenues rise above pre–Hurricane Katrina figures.

PUTTING IT ALL TOGETHER: FACTORS USED IN CONSUMER BEHAVIOR AND DECISION MAKING

On average, the number of leisure room nights is steadily increasing, especially in the baby boomer and Generation X segments, and better yet, travelers are going back to longer leisure stays. Multigenerational vacationers, for example, require a greater variety of amenities for all age groups. The trend is toward the consumers' inclusion of cultural experiences on their trips. However, Generation X leisure travelers are looking for the most "untouched, exotic, authentic, and remote" locations. Intimate atmospheres and personalization in products and service are important to them, so it is difficult to obtain repeat visits from them. On the other hand, value-added packaged vacations continue to be strong for all leisure travelers. Some gambling destinations, especially Las Vegas, had experienced a significant expansion of smaller, more personalized non-casino hotels. Some guests may prefer staying in non-casino properties to avoid the "factory-like" mass tourism experience perceived at the mega-gambling resorts.

The current market focus has switched to the higher-yielding upscale gambling market, with an emphasis on supporting upscale services such as designer-label shopping and gourmet restaurants. So, to attract visitors, the purchase channel of choice for the emerging leisure travel segments is the Internet. To attract these visitors, you could create a Web site that draws repeat guests with new, unique, and changing offers with value.

Younger generations have a completely different world perspective than boomers do. The average Nintendo user of yesterday is 29 years old today, gets bored easily, and is less "tradition" oriented. For example, younger consumers have a higher propensity for more intellectually challenging casino table games, while older gamblers are more likely to choose slot machines.

Retirement at age 65 is also coming to an end because of the rise of pension problems and the fact that people are healthier and more active than they used to be. As a result, many people over 65 want to continue to work, and the fact is that the skills of older people are needed in the marketplace. Although this trend could work in favor of casinos because of an expanded labor pool of potential employees, the overall impact could be negative as seniors represent a significant portion of casino consumers.

However, despite all the consumer behavior information and trends, fundamentally, a casino is a casino. Some have new, different games, but casino floors feel and sound pretty much the same. So, the question is: "Why do consumers pick one casino over another?" Part of the reason is the concept of **player's clubs**. The casinos have developed a way of tracking each player so the casino can offer comps to get gamblers into the system. However, a player may be a member of more than one casino's player's club. As a result, many different casinos send their newsletters and coupons to the same person. This creates a consumer who is a smarter, more value-oriented casino "comp" shopper.

How do casinos win customer loyalty? How can they differentiate their "house" from the other "houses" on the block? Service. Every casino has tables, slots, restrooms, and bars. Most have a buffet for a quick bite to eat and a clean room for the night. These are the basic expectations that a person assumes will be met. For example, on one trip we checked into the hotel for the night and went upstairs to unpack before venturing into the casino. The room was clean, but the cigarette smoke odor was so strong that we could hardly breathe. Luckily, we were able to get a smoke-free room and we made the switch. What would have happened if the front desk had told us that there were no nonsmoking rooms available? What would we do? We would have immediately checked out and never returned. This illustration points out the problems when basic expectations are not met. Most of the time, a player moves on to the next casino and never looks back.

Suppose that during this routine stay the staff is friendlier and the operations are more efficient and better run than the casino next door. What value would be added to this experience? For example, an elderly woman freezes at the escalator. Impatient irate people begin to form a line waiting for her to move. What would you do? One quick-thinking security person walked over with a big smile, offered her hand, and asked, "Need company?" She proceeded to help the woman onto the first step and then rode down with her. As they chatted and laughed, the elderly woman relaxed and got off the escalator without any problem. How would this incident affect her decision the next time? Do you think she will be more likely to go back to the friendly casino with the nice security person?

Conclusion

Knowledge of consumer behaviors is critical for the casino gaming industry to tailor products and services that will appeal to casino gamblers. Conversely, this information also provides valuable insights on what types of communications, lifestyle, values, attitudes, and behaviors that would be viewed negatively by casino gamblers. Knowing what "turns on" and "turns off" the casino gambling consumer is critical for the success of the casino industry. Casino marketers can use this demographic and psychographic information to establish the optimum mix of products and services for casino gamblers. Savvy casino industry operators monitor overall consumer behavior trends very carefully for cues in maintaining and developing new marketing and operational strategies.

Many consumer behavior trends can be observed from simple observation of emerging societal trends. For example, the current popularity of so-called reality shows on television is probably an excellent indicator of a major groundswell of public interest in forms of escapism from the realities of an increasingly complicated world environment. Casino gambling is well positioned to take advantage of this same trend toward escapism as casinos offer respite from the real world. Have you ever tried to find a clock in a casino? The reason that clocks are not found anywhere inside a casino is that operators do not want casino patrons to know what time it is,

as perceived time shortages might prompt a patron to finish playing and focus instead on a non-casino–related activity such as work or family obligations.

Casino marketers must understand the underlying needs, wants, motivations, and aspirations of their patrons. These changes can be affected by many factors, including demographic variables such as age, income, occupation, education level, place of residency, and so on. Changes can also be affected by numerous psychographic factors such as motivations, aspirations, lifestyle, and beliefs.

Consumers are also faced with an ever-expanding plethora of choices in their everyday leisure activities. Casino marketers must compete with all other forms of leisure activities, including hobbies, shopping, sports, and other travel-related options. Additionally, consumers can now also visit online casinos available 24 hours a day to anyone with an Internet connection. For consumers unable to access the Internet, new services are rapidly becoming available where cellular telephones can be used for casino gaming by using a combination of the telephone number keypad and the visual display screen.

Casino operators who establish superior competencies in the domain of consumer behavior will have a significant competitive advantage over peer operators who lack this critical skill set.

Key Words

Consumer behavior 39	Compulsive gamblers 45	Psychographics 46
Cognitive dissonance 40	Occupational gamblers 45	Player's club 49
Utility of wealth theory 42	Recreational gamblers 45	
Variable schedule of reinforcement 44		

Review Questions

1. In the study of consumer behavior, which aspects of purchase decisions are considered?
2. What does the study of consumer behavior begin with?
3. What are the four stages of the consumer decision-making process?
4. The majority of consumer behavior research in the casino gambling field has been based on the study of which five subdisciplines?
5. Why do sociologists study gambling?
6. What are the two simplest theories offered by the field of psychology as to why people gamble and why they chase after losses?
7. Motives for gambling can be broadly categorized into three general groups; what are they?
8. Which income brackets of Americans have the highest casino gambling participation rates, and which income brackets have the lowest?
9. Which segment of gambler offers casino marketers the greatest future potential of market expansion compared to the other two segments?
10. Why do consumers pick one casino over another?
11. How do casinos win customer loyalty? How can they differentiate their "house" from the other "houses" on the block?
12. What is the reason that clocks are not found anywhere inside a casino?

Endnotes

1. Some of the chapter was first introduced in Hashimoto, K. (1998). Consumer Behavior. In Hashimoto, K., Kline, S. F., & Fenich, G. G. *Casino Management: Past-Present-Future*. Dubuque: Kendall Hunt Publishing.
2. American Gaming Association's (AGA) (2005). State of the States Annual Report.
3. American Gaming Association's (AGA) (2008). State of the States Annual Report. Accessed on June 15, 2008, http://www.americangaming.org/assets/files/aga_2008_sos.pdf.
4. Ibid.
5. Cohen, J. (1988). Explaining Gambling Behavior. In Rosecrance, John (Ed.), *Gambling Without Guilt: The Legitimation of an American Pastime*. Pacific Grove: Brooks/Cole Publishing Co., 53–70.
6. Ibid.
7. Ibid.
8. Ibid
9. Ibid.
10. Unknown (2004). Profile of the American Casino Gambler: Harrah's Survey 2004. Accessed on November 21, 2004, http://www.hotel-online.com/News/PR2004_4th/Oct04_HarrahsSurvey.html.
11. http://www.harrahs.com/images/PDFs/Profile_Survey_2006.pdf. Accessed on January 11, 2007.
12. Lowenhar, J. & Boykin, S. (1995). Casino Gaming Behavior and the Psychology of Winning and Losing: How Gamers Overcome Persistent Failure. In Eadington, W. (Ed.), *The Gambling Studies: Proceedings of the Sixth National Conference on Gambling and Risk Taking*. Reno: Institute for the Study of Gambling and Commercial Gaming, 182–205.
13. American Gaming Association's (AGA) (2008). State of the States Annual Report. Accessed on June 15, 2008, http://www.americangaming.org/assets/files/aga_2008_sos.pdf.

CHAPTER 5

BEYOND THE TRADITIONAL GAMBLER

MEETINGS AND CONVENTIONS

GEORGE G. FENICH

Learning Objectives

1. To explore the history of the contrasting relationship between casinos and conventioneers[1]

2. To understand the history of the lack of convention business in pre-1990 gaming destinations

3. To learn how casinos in Las Vegas and Atlantic City began to look to conventions to increase their income

4. To learn about the role of hosts in the meetings and conventions industry

5. To learn about the role of venues in the meetings and conventions industry

6. To understand the role of information sources in the meetings and conventions industry

7. To understand the role of coordination in the meetings and conventions industry

8. To learn about new and expanded conventions and meeting facilities in the Las Vegas area

9. To learn about new and expanded conventions and meeting facilities in the Atlantic City area

10. To learn about new and expanded conventions and meeting facilities in the Mississippi Gulf Coast area

11. To learn of new and expanded conventions and meeting facilities in Native American casinos

Chapter Outline

INTRODUCTION

The casino industry has always relied on the leisure traveler whose primary motivation is to gamble. Thus, one would expect the casino and convention industries to operate in totally different arenas since conventioneers go to meetings all day. This was true until the mid-1990s. Today, the casino industry is embracing the convention industry and constructing facilities to meet the needs of convention and meeting attendees.

This chapter begins by establishing the background for this historical separation of the two industries by putting forth the history of casino gaming in the United States. This is followed by a review of how and why there was a lack of convention/meeting business in both Las Vegas and Atlantic City. The chapter then moves on to an in-depth analysis of the evolution of the meeting/convention business in Las Vegas, Atlantic City, and other jurisdictions. From there, we will discuss an overview of the meetings and events industry with a discussion of the new meetings and conventions additions to all the casinos.

CASINOS AND CONVENTIONEERS: NOT PERFECT TOGETHER

In the past, the casino industry elicited images of megaresorts, top-notch entertainment, inexpensive buffet meals, comp rooms, and people who gamble all night and sleep all day.

As can be seen from this image, casinos have historically targeted the leisure consumer for the majority of their business. Everything the casino did was based on the viewpoint that customers must be involved in gambling during most of their stay. This was due to the widely held belief that a casino could be successful only if it derived virtually all its revenue from the casino floor. One only needs to look at the early hotel rooms found in casinos where the furnishings were relatively Spartan and even the cable TV had a minimum number of channels. This was done with the purpose of motivating the leisure traveler to get out of the hotel room and onto the casino floor.

This was fine so long as Las Vegas was a monopoly. However in 1976, Atlantic City legalized casino gaming. The legislation mandated that all casinos be integral parts of full service hotels. However, since the managers were all trained in Las Vegas, they maintained the old traditions and belief that "The only path to success and profits lies in generating revenue on the casino floor." Therefore, the target market for a casino consists of the

FIGURE 5.1 Circus Circus has always catered to families with its huge neon-lit clown beckoning visitors and locals.

Source: Alan Keohane © Dorling Kindersley.

people who come to gamble as their primary recreation. This perspective was fine even with the two giants (Las Vegas and Atlantic City) of gambling because there are a lot of people who live in the United States. There was certainly enough to go around.

However, by the 1990s, the two Meccas of casino gaming began to be concerned. Increasing competition from riverboat gambling, new land-based casinos, and Native American gambling venues were cropping up all over America. This generated fear of a potential market saturation for gaming. Adding to this problem was the fact that both Atlantic City and, especially, Las Vegas were increasing the number of casinos and hotel rooms, thus creating internal competition. Further, none of their strategies, such as trying to attract families in the late 1980s, were particularly successful.

Adding to the confusion, these new casinos had a new perspective on the importance of attracting gamblers. The new gambling regions wanted to have a complete entertainment-recreation area. However, they realized that gambling would be a quick, easy cash cow to acquire the money for this development as well as a related attraction. So the first step was to open a casino or a riverboat to begin development. The casino would be the initial reason why tourists came to the area, but eventually as the recreation and entertainment venues were developed, gambling would be another reason to come. All of these reasons forced operators to become competitive and look for other sources of business. Also, casino management began to realize that there were potential profit centers outside the casino floor in the form of hotel rooms, food and beverage, shopping, and other amenities.

THE LACK OF CONVENTION BUSINESS IN PRE-1990 GAMING DESTINATIONS

The traits and behaviors of conventioneers were not of interest to casino operators because these operators believed that conventioneers would take advantage of the amenities casinos had to offer without gambling enough. Therefore, meeting and convention attendees were not even on the radar screen of the operators since the attendees did not fit the demographic and psychographic profile of the casino patron. However, when business was slow, the casino hotel might grant a meeting planner rooms for their convention. After all, some business was good during a slow season. On the other hand, if there was an influx of gamblers at that same time, a casino operator had no compunction about calling and canceling the rooms at the last minute. "I have actually been told in so many words, 'We don't need your business' says Debbie Hubler . . . of the National Cattlemen's Beef Association in Englewood, Colorado."[2]

After all, conventioneers had almost the exact opposite of the psychographics and demographics of gamblers. Unlike the gamblers who spend all of their time at the tables, conventioneers are in meetings all day, want a nice dinner, are not particularly price conscious about rooms, and tend to be conservative with their money. Therefore, "there was a long period when the leadership of the casino industry did not subscribe to the importance of the convention trade."[3] However, given its proximity to a large drive-in market, gamblers in Atlantic City usually came on the weekends, casinos considered filling some rooms with conventioneers, but only in mid-week. "Traditionally, the big hotels are forced to offer mid-week bargain packages to fill rooms Monday through Thursday. This, of course, affects bottom line."[4] However, casino managers who considered hosting a convention/meeting would only do so during these slow periods when they felt it was impossible to attract the core gambler. In Atlantic City, this meant that conventions/meetings were relegated to the winter months when chilling temperatures and howling winds made it very unpleasant to even be in Atlantic City. The authors remember scheduling a national conference in Atlantic City during early January. A major snowstorm that paralyzed the city for three days began the day before the conference was to begin and wreaked havoc with the meeting. In addition, casino managers could not even envision offsetting lower gaming revenues from meeting/convention attendees with higher room rates or food and beverage business. "We have had all these rooms, and we haven't been able to migrate to the high price midweek segment. The convention business has been starkly missing from our customer profile."[5]

LAS VEGAS AND ATLANTIC CITY LOOK TO CONVENTIONS

Destinations that focused largely on casino gaming have only recently begun to look to the conventions and meetings segment as a significant source of business and revenue. Even though Las Vegas has been a travel destination since at least the 1940s, the boom in convention/meeting business, with its commensurate construction, did not take off until the mid-1990s. According to Yaskin, "In a perfect casino world . . . executives could close every sales office and fill every room with gamblers, but that isn't reality. And so, in order to fill premium rooms and suites with high-end clientele, the casino markets look to convention and business travelers.[6] While casino operators have clearly not abandoned the high roller and individual tourist markets, many are making concerted efforts to cultivate the meeting business with incentives and other initiatives."[7]

This is a distinct change since until recently all but two Las Vegas "casino operators have considered meetings only as midweek filler when business is low. Now everyone is realizing there are dollars in the market."[8]

> . . . within a chips' throw of every gaming Mecca lies a convention center—the distant cousin to the nuclear family of gambling tourism. Everybody knows they're related but they just can't quite agree as to how. It's an uneasy relationship, at

FIGURE 5.2   G2E is the largest casino industry trade show.

best. . . . But across the years meeting planners have felt as if they've been tossed the table scraps by the surrounding hotels that would really rather keep their rooms available just in case a high roller should stumble in.[9]

Conventions/meetings are a good source of business for casinos because they complement, not compete with, the leisure gambler. Gamblers prefer to go to casinos on weekends, holidays, and summer periods, just like most leisure travelers. By contrast, conventions/meetings rarely start their program prior to Monday and prefer to complete activities by Thursday so attendees can be at home with their families on the weekends. The same holds true for holidays and summers; most groups do not meet then. As a result, conventions/meetings fit nicely with the ebb and flow of casino clientele.

Additionally, as casino operations became more corporate in their workings, they "crunched the numbers" to ascertain opportunities. They found that conventions and meetings could be a good source of business. They calculated that these attendees had larger pocketbooks and were not as rate conscious as traditional gamblers. Thus, casino hotels could charge attendees a higher room rate than leisure-based gamblers and counteract the diminished gaming revenues from those attendees. They also determined that the convention/meeting business could generate additional revenues channeled through the food and beverage department. Unlike the leisure gambler, conventions/meetings would spend money on full-priced food and beverage and the convention/meeting sponsor would pay for banquets, receptions, coffee breaks, and more. The companies that exhibit at trade shows also spend large sums entertaining attendees and clients at hospitality suites, elaborate dinners, and receptions.

The "yield managers" and financial analysts of casino corporations figured out that conventions/meetings could generate more, overall, than the average gambler. The corporate headquarters of casino companies convinced the property level

FIGURE 5.3 Conventions and trade shows draw many tourists to town who may not have visited before.

managers of the importance of the convention/meeting segment. "From the glitzy boulevards of Las Vegas to the lower reaches of the Mississippi Delta, properties that woo groups on the twin strengths of convention facilities and casinos are multiplying and expanding at a rapid rate."[10]

OVERVIEW OF THE MEETINGS AND EVENTS INDUSTRY

People appear to have an inherent need for social interactions. This need, whether expressed for survival or for entertainment, has been the underlying foundation of an industry. However, the idea of people meeting is so common, that no one actually thinks of it as an industry where people actually work and make money. While meetings and events have been part of people's lives throughout recorded history, the government did not even list "meeting planner" as a recognized profession (in the Standard Industry Classification codes) until the late 1980s. At the last count, the Convention Industry Council (**CIC**) consists of 32 organizational members representing more than 100,000 individuals.[11]

The meetings and events industry has three different groups. Meeting planners are the ones who actually put together meetings and events and they are employed by associations, corporations, and governments. The organizations that provide the services for the meetings and events also host their own events. In the casinos for example, they can provide in-house meeting planning services for their customers along with the space and amenities that are required. The third group is of course the most important: the attendees.

For people who want to learn some of the terminology, the Convention Industry Council provides an online glossary of terms and phrases called **APEX** (Accepted Practices Exchange).

Types of Meetings and Events

Generally, the industry consists of meetings, conferences, conventions, trade shows, special events, sport-related events, celebrations, and other types. "Meeting" is defined in the APEX glossary as, "An event where the primary activity of the attendees is to attend educational sessions, participate in meetings/discussions, socialize, or attend other organized events. There is no exhibit component to this event."[12] The APEX glossary defines "events" as those held for entertainment purposes such as weddings. Events that are held for special occasions, rather than held on a regular, often annual basis, are known as "special events." Events vary in terms of duration from hours to weeks, and in terms of size. Some events can be as large as a presidential inauguration or a movie star's wedding. Some charge admission fees to help cover expenses, while others, like weddings, are offered free to all participants with expenses being covered by the host.

"Conventions" are a specific kind of meeting. One aspect of a convention is a meeting where business and/or educational sessions are provided. Conventions can also include a trade show or exposition as part of the meeting. Trade shows are larger areas where exhibitors provide demonstrations of their products and answer questions from convention attendees. At G2E (Global Gaming Expo) there are educational workshops during the morning followed by a lunch with either a keynote speaker or a ceremony with industry awards. Then in the afternoon, the trade show floor opens for attendees and industry people. The trade show is not open to the public. When a meeting is used to conduct business and to provide educational opportunities, but no exhibition or trade show is available, that meeting is often known as a "conference"; however many people use this term very loosely.

FIGURE 5.4   Conferences need registration areas outside of the meeting space.

Hosts

Generally, associations and corporations host these gatherings. Associations are nonprofit and formed for specific purposes. The not-for-profit designation allows the association to not pay income taxes, and in some designations their members are exempt as well when they contribute to the association. Generally, associations can be classified as **SMERF** (social, military, ethnic, religious, and fraternal) organizations. As a rule, these groups and the members tend to be careful with their limited budgets. A common goal is to educate their members on their common interests. As a result, they hold small board meetings, regional sessions, and annual conferences where they bring everyone together to network and attract new members. Quite often, the annual conference's profits support the activities of the association.

Corporations hold numerous meetings for employees, customers, and independent sales representatives. Corporate meetings tend to promote products, services, or ideas in order to increase their product knowledge while pumping up employee motivation and productivity.

Venues

Convention centers provide exhibit space for meetings that need large areas for trade shows or expositions. In addition, most gatherings need a ballroom, a registration area, and a dining hall, at a minimum. Convention centers tend to have extremely versatile space that can be converted from a large, open room with 20,000 to 100,000 square feet of uninterrupted floor space, to several rooms separated by partitions or temporary walls. Most conventions offer beverages during the course of the day and sometimes light food like fruit or pastries.

FIGURE 5.5   Corporate meeting rooms can be very elegant.

Conference centers are generally smaller facilities that cater to meetings that do not need large exhibitor areas. Typically, they have break-out rooms that allow the large group to divide into smaller groups. These rooms usually have special hookups for computers, projection, DVD, and other equipment to provide presenters hi-tech access to their materials.

Information Sources

Quite often, someone from the association or corporation will contact the locale's chamber of commerce, a convention and visitors bureau (**CVB**), or a government agency in that area. These are collectively known as destination marketing organizations (**DMO**). Therefore, many businesses in the area will be members of a DMO in order to have the latest information on what groups are coming to town and who the contact person is. This allows casinos to contact prospective clients directly and offer their services. On the other hand, a destination management company (**DMC**) is usually a corporation that works with a distant host organization to plan a meeting or event. An independent event planner can be located in a small town and still plan special events in other states and cities like Las Vegas or Atlantic City. This independent planner might subcontract with a DMC in one of these locations. The independent planner develops a contract for services to be provided and is paid by the host organization.

Some services, such as volunteer recruitment and management, might be provided by the local DMO, CVB, or DMC. Registration services can be provided by suppliers skilled in this function and will include online marketing materials; registration databases; online payments; on-site registration handling; and reports provided before, during, and after the meeting or event. Other services provided for meetings and events typically fall under the broader category known as "suppliers."

Coordination

Besides coordinating the efforts of a planning team, meeting and event planners are also responsible for details. They develop the event specifications guide (**ESG**), which includes all of the details necessary for running a smooth meeting. The Convention Industry Council created a template for the ESG that can be found at http://www.conventionindustry.org/apex. Typically, the next step is to send out an **RFP** (request for proposal), specifying the projected purpose, goals, projected attendance figures, agenda, hotel, dining, and other requirements for the meeting. The RFPs are very specific and help the selection committee or planner decide which of the sites are the top contenders for their business. Once the list is narrowed, planners and selection committee members often visit the site to assess the location to see if it is suitable for their needs. Once the specific location is selected, the meeting planner develops the detailed contracts for costs and facilities.

Planning a meeting or event may take only days or as long as years. Associations tend to begin planning their annual events five or more years in advance. On the other hand, corporations tend to take weeks or months. The meeting planner rarely works alone, and may be responsible for coordinating the efforts of numerous contracts and several committees who review these contracts across various aspects of the meeting or event. Once the planner's responsibilities for registration, food and drink, and other duties are successfully handled, then the final step is to prepare an evaluation of the suppliers and the overall success of the meeting.

Meetings and conventions encompass numerous types of activities that result when more than two people get together to be entertained, educated, informed, or to practice skills. There can be planners for small meetings or giant conventions with trade shows. The three largest hosts of these meetings are associations, corporations, and government agencies. Services and suppliers to the meetings and events industry generally involve marketing, transportation, audio/visual components, atmosphere, food and beverage, entertainment, and speakers. Meetings and conventions are big business. However, casinos historically rejected their business. Now with revenue management crunching the numbers, managers are realizing the new profit potential of conventioneers.

NEW OR EXPANDED FACILITIES

Many existing casino hotels are adding, expanding, or renovating their convention/meeting space. Bally's Las Vegas began renovation by updating its meeting space to 175,000 square feet. Caesars Palace, once the exclusive haunt of high rollers, added 110,000 square feet of function space in 1997, then increased its meeting space by 86,000 square feet in 2005, bringing the resort total to an impressive 240,000. The MGM Grand hotel and casino (originally with a leisure-oriented Wizard of Oz theme) built a 380,000 square-foot conference center in 1998, and in 2002 closed its theme park to all but convention groups. Even some of the casino hotels built since the mid-1990s are adding convention/meeting space. Mandalay Bay Resort added a 1.7 million square-foot convention center to become the fifth largest center in the United States. This was done in an effort to level out the swings in their mid-week and weekend business.[13] This is in addition to their existing 190,000 square foot conference center. Executives said they would like to see "40 percent of their hotel business coming from conventioneers and trade show goers, rather than the current 21 percent that mix constitutes."[14]

The Venetian is the first hotel in the history of the world's entertainment capital to cater almost exclusively to the convention trade. All 3,000 rooms in the main tower are suites and all are linked to the 1.7 million square feet of space at the Sands Expo and Convention Center.[15]

"The Sands Expo center is the largest, privately owned convention facility in the country and one of the top five in total size. A major expansion was announced in early 2008 that would add an additional floor to the existing facility and build a new 2 million square-foot exhibition center. The new center would actually replace the existing one, thus allowing the construction of 7,000 more hotel rooms on the site of the older center. And I think the Venetian and Las Vegas are taking a share of the convention business from smaller cities like Nashville and Dallas."—Bank of America analyst Andrew Susser.[16]

Las Vegas Conventions and Attendance

Las Vegas has become the biggest convention city in the United States, surpassing Chicago and New York. Las Vegas has a total of about 9.7 million square feet of convention/meeting space, and 137,000 hotel rooms. According to the Las Vegas Convention and Visitor Authority, in 2007, the city hosted about 23,000 conventions and trade shows with 6.2 million attendees, resulting in an economic impact of $8.5 billion. Generally, conventioneers spend half

FIGURE 5.6   Entrance to the Las Vegas Convention Center.

a day longer than tourists (4.1 nights compared to 3.7 nights). Further, trade show delegates spent an average of $1,273 on nongaming items while conventioneers spent $961. This compares to only $630 for tourists.[17] Of the travelers to Las Vegas, the same percentage of people said they came to gamble as came for a meeting or convention (12%).

In spite of these numbers, which gives the appearance that Las Vegas is one of America's top convention and trade show destinations, it could do much more. According to Sheldon Anderson, chairman of the Venetian Casino Hotel, Las Vegas has not yet tapped one half of one percent of the convention business. He said he "battled with some Las Vegas officials about the importance of the convention business in past years and believes that business is now more important than ever as the city seeks to continually fill more hotel rooms."[18]

DEVELOPMENT IN ATLANTIC CITY

Like Las Vegas, Atlantic City casino/hotel operators historically focused on the leisure gambler as the primary source of business. This occurred in spite of the fact that Atlantic City was one of the first municipalities to stage a national special event, the Miss America Pageant. The old mindset died hard, but it did change. In the late 1990s, Atlantic City operators, along with elected officials, decided to embrace the convention and meeting business. According to Joe DiGirolamo, vice president of convention development for the Atlantic City Convention and Visitors Authority: "Although casino development is the linchpin of Atlantic City's fortunes, the convention industry is critical to the city's growth."[19] There was a long period when the leadership of the casino industry did not subscribe to the importance of the convention trade.[20] Further, it was only in 1993 that the state-run Casino Reinvestment Authority began to offer financing for hotel construction, but only if operators would commit a percentage of those rooms for convention blocks.[21]

Probably the most significant physical development was the new convention center, meant to replace the aging event hall located on the boardwalk. The new facility opened in 1997 at a cost of $268 million, with half a million square feet of space, and 45 meeting rooms. It has more contiguous floor space than any competing convention center between Boston and Atlanta. Interestingly, it is not located on the boardwalk with the casinos but is on the opposite side of the island at the foot of the Atlantic City Expressway and adjacent to the rail and bus terminal. A non-casino hotel has been built next to the new center that has 502 rooms, a 16,000 square-foot ballroom, and 5,000 square feet of pre-function space. The Washington-based association NCEA, whose show attracts 14,000 attendees, exemplifies the previous lack, or deterioration of the convention trade and the subsequent success of the center. They had not met in Atlantic City since 1975 but are moving their show back to the city because of its new center.[22] "We are no longer a one-dimensional casino town," says Gary Musich, vice president of convention development for the Atlantic City Convention and Visitors Authority, "and with our many high-quality non-gaming attributes, planners and groups have enough well-rounded agenda choices to comfortably fill a three- to four-day visit."[23]

Atlantic City saw almost no casino/hotel construction in the decade of the 1990s. However, there are three new casinos by MGM Grand, Steve Wynn, and a partnership between Mirage and Boyd Gaming. The Borgata opened with 18,000 square feet of meeting space. "The casino industry is now very aggressively developing Atlantic City's convention capacity."[24] Thus, it is clear that after 20 years as a gaming destination "Atlantic City is pushing to reclaim its former status as one of America's top convention destinations."[25]

DEVELOPMENT IN OTHER JURISDICTIONS

This chapter has focused on casinos and conventions in Las Vegas and Atlantic City. The reason for this focus is that those two destinations are, by far, the most notable casino communities in the United States. Thus, they are the most representative of the relationship between casinos and conventions/meetings. However, during the 1990s other jurisdictions have legalized gaming, and their relationship with conventions/meetings has followed the pattern of Las Vegas and Atlantic City.

Development on the Mississippi Gulf Coast

After Las Vegas and Atlantic City, the largest concentration of casinos is along the Mississippi Gulf Coast in the communities of Biloxi and Gulfport, where casino gaming was legalized in 1990. "Casinos no longer live by gaming alone," says Tim Hinckley, vice president of marketing for Isle of Capri Casinos.[26] The Mississippi Gulf Coast was devastated when Hurricane Katrina wiped out most structures and physical improvements. In order to stimulate rebuilding, the state of Mississippi relaxed the laws governing casino development. The result was that "casinos" no longer had to be on barges over the water but could be built a few hundred yards inland—on solid ground. This change is expected to spur development, much of which will include convention/event/meeting space. Tourism officials are hoping to attract more meetings to the Gulf Coast to counteract the saturation of the gaming market. "This is certainly a market that will continue to increase its attraction to group business."[27]

The newest casino hotel, Beau Rivage, reopened in August of 2006 after being dev-astated by Hurricane Katrina. It has 1,740 guest rooms, features a 50,000 square-foot convention center, and has a 17,000 square-foot ballroom that can accommodate 1,800 conventioneers. The Hollywood Casino has 17,000 square feet of meeting space while the IP Casino Resort has 18,000 square feet. Under construction and due to open in 2010 is the Margaritaville Resort and Casino that will have 66,000 square feet of meeting space and almost 800 guest rooms.

Bayview Ventures LLC has proposed a new $325 million resort development on the Biloxi Back Bay area east of Boomtown Casino on 7.9 acres of land. The Mississippi Gaming Commission approved the site plan in March 2008. Plans call for a 519-room hotel, 70,000 square feet of gaming space, 1,400 slot machines, 45 table games, 4 restaurants, a swimming pool and spa, shopping, an entertainment venue with 2,000 seats, and a 25,000 square-foot meeting and banquet facility. Ground breaking could take place in late 2008. Also proposed is the Broadwater, a $1 billion project which will consist of 2 casinos; 3,375 condo units; 1,900 hotel rooms; a 180-acre, 18-hole golf course; 585,000 square-foot retail entertainment space; 125,000 square-foot gaming floor; 104,000 square-foot convention space; and a marina. The Mississippi Gulf Coast has followed the lead of other gaming jurisdictions in trying to embrace the meetings and conventions market.

Native American Casinos

Native Americans obtained the right to operate casinos in 1987 as a result of a Supreme Court ruling called the Indian Gaming Regulatory Act. The first Native American casino hotel to open was **Foxwoods** in Connecticut in 1992. When it was first developed, it only had a small 280 room hotel and no meeting space, but relied on the casino to attract leisure travelers from the northeast corridor of the United States. A museum was added in 1998 and the operators were surprised when it attracted groups and corporations who held meetings there. Today, Foxwoods has over 1,400 rooms with 170,000 square feet of meeting space, including a ballroom with seating for 1,800. "Foxwoods currently hosts 150 to 200 meetings a year, primarily for Northeast based groups."[28]

Following the success of Foxwoods, Mohegan Sun opened in the same state in 1996. They also had little meeting space when they opened, but now have an $800 million expansion that includes 100,000 square feet of meeting space. "This isn't being built as a hotel with casino attached," says David Casey, vice president of sales and marketing, "It is being built as a meetings and events destination."[29]

Some other notable Native American casinos with convention space include:

- *Mystic Lake Resort & Casino, Prior Lake, Minnesota*   Located about 25 minutes from downtown Minneapolis, this property, owned and operated by the Shakopee Mdewakanton Sioux Community, is surrounded by a population of at least three million within an hour's drive and contains the Midwest's largest casino (it's also the official casino hotel of the Mall of America). Mystic Lake offers a 600-room hotel and 21,000 square feet of meeting space; its largest ballroom seats 750 theater style, but a 2,000-seat entertainment center is also available for meetings.
- *Seminole Hard Rock Hotel & Casino, Hollywood, Florida*   This may be the most likely candidate to compete with Mohegan Sun or Foxwoods, Sherf predicts, because of its population density (the property is just a half-hour from Miami), lack of competition,

FIGURE 5.7 Aerial view of the Mashantucket Pequot Indian Reservation in Ledyard, Connecticut, where Foxwoods Resort Casino nestles in the woods.

Source: Bob Child/AP Wide World Photos.

and the fact that the Seminole tribe's compact with the state has no limits on growth. This sprawling, 86-acre resort offers a 500-room hotel, a 130,000 square-foot casino, and more than 60,000 square feet of meeting space.

- *Seneca Niagara Casino & Hotel, Niagara Falls, New York*   Located just blocks away from Niagara Falls and with a population of more than six million living within a three-hour drive, this property attracts gamers from as far away as Pittsburgh and Cleveland. And with the completion of a $200-million, 604-room hotel (the largest in western New York), Seneca Niagara is betting that it can parlay its successful casino business into a viable meetings destination. Besides six restaurants, the property offers 35,000 square feet of meeting space, including an event center with capacity for up to 2,200.

As can be seen, many Native American gaming venues throughout the United States have developed not only into full-scale resorts but are also focusing on attracting a large number of convention and meeting attendees. They are following the successful strategy of non-Native American casino operators. They are taking advantage of their location by bringing in groups that lack the budget to travel to Las Vegas. Planners are benefiting from this approach with more meeting venues to choose from.

Conclusion

The United States has had legalized casinos for three-quarters of a century. During that period, casino operators relied almost exclusively on leisure gamblers to generate business. They were too focused on their "core" gambler to realize there were other opportunities. This all changed in the 1980s and 1990s as gaming was legalized in more and more destinations, and that caused concern about competition, saturation, and cannibalization. While casinos tried many strategies to broaden their draw beyond the "traditional gambler," the attempts did not work as well as anticipated.

The one strategy that is successful for casino operators in the United States is the targeting of the meetings and convention segments. The success of this approach is seen from coast to coast in places like Las Vegas, Atlantic City, Connecticut, and Native American tribal lands. The strategy works well for a number of reasons. First, casino operators, or more specifically the research analysts at corporate headquarters, determined that meeting/convention attendees could contribute as much as gamblers to the bottom line. This is accomplished through a higher room rate, extensive food and beverage or catering revenue, and a longer length of stay. However, meeting and convention attendees spend less on the gaming floor. This is in keeping with the new trends toward making the hotel, along with food and beverage, profit centers. In addition, casino operators determined that high rollers did not want to eat at buffets, but wanted outstanding food and beverage outlets. Since the casinos had already begun adding names like Wolfgang Puck and Emeril's to their amenities, this coincided nicely with the needs of conventioneers. Other additions included retail outlets that are frequented as much by conventioneers as by gamblers. Further, conventioneers prefer to have their events during mid-week and non-holiday periods that are exactly the opposite of the mainstream gambler. Thus, there is a symbiotic relationship between the casino and convention industries.

The attraction of conventions/meetings to casino destinations is a recent phenomenon that is only now taking hold. Virtually all of the new, billion-dollar resorts being planned in Las Vegas include significant amounts of meeting and convention space. Given the newness of this phenomenon, there is every reason to believe that this trend will continue long into the future.

Key Words

CIC *57*	CVB *60*	ESG *60*
APEX *57*	DMO *60*	RFP *60*
SMERF *59*	DMC *60*	Foxwoods *64*

Review Questions

1. Explain the history of the contrasting relationship between casinos and conventioneers.
2. Explain the history of the lack of convention business in pre-1990 gaming destinations.
3. Detail how casinos in Las Vegas and Atlantic City began to look to conventions to increase their income.
4. Discuss the role of hosts in the meetings and conventions industry.
5. Discuss the role of venues in the meetings and conventions industry.
6. Discuss the role of information sources in the meetings and conventions industry.
7. Discuss the role of coordination in the meetings and conventions industry.
8. Detail the rise of new and expanded conventions and meeting facilities in the Las Vegas area.
9. Detail the rise of new and expanded conventions and meeting facilities in the Atlantic City area.
10. Detail the rise of new and expanded conventions and meeting facilities in the Mississippi Gulf Coast area.
11. Detail the rise of new and expanded conventions and meeting facilities in Native American casinos.

Bibliography

Baker, T. "New Games in Town." *Meetings & Conventions* 37, no. 7 (June 2002): 43–52.

Bulavsky, J. "Upscale Shops for Thousands of Conventioneers." *Casino Journal* XII, no. 6 (June 1999): 57.

Fisher, M. G. "A Wynn-Win Situation." *Successful Meetings* (April 2001): 67–73.

Hanson, B., and Kline, K. "Developers Placing Big Bets in Las Vegas and Atlantic City." *Convene* XII, no. 4 (May 1997): 75–77.

Hardin, T. "It's a Push." *Successful Meetings*, 87–93.

Ligos, M., and Meyers, C. "If It's Tuesday . . . It Must Be Paris . . . or Venice, or New York, or Even Myanmar—If You Happen to be in Las Vegas that Is." *Successful Meetings* (April 2000): 69–72.

Palermo, D. "Southern Saturation." *International Gaming and Wagering Business* 22, no. 5 (May 2001): 13–17.

Ross, J. R. "Associations Betting on Attendance Appeal of Gaming Destinations." *Convene* XIII, no. 4 (May 1998): 81–86.

Shure, P. "Counting Convention Delegates." *Convene* XII, no. 4 (May 1997): 42–43.

———. "Largest Shows." *Convene*, Special Issue (November 2000), 24–27.

Sullivan, C. K. "'Tis the Season." *Successful Meetings* (April 2001): 91–95.

Teitler, A. D., and Baker, T. "Feeling Lucky." *Meetings & Conventions* 35, no. 7 (June 2000): 47–54.

Weinert, J. "Destination: Atlantic City." *International Gaming and Wagering Business* 23, no. 9 (September 2002): 20–22.

Endnotes

1. NOTE: Much of the information in this chapter is based on: Fenich, G. G. & Hashimoto, K. (2004). "Casinos and Conventions: Strange Bedfellows." *Journal of Convention and Event Tourism,* 6(1/2), 63–80.

2. Finney, M. I. (1997, March). High stakes relationships: casinos and conventions. *Association Management*, 49(3), 64–66.

3. (Ghitelman, 1997:79).

4. Shemeligian, B. (1999, July). The new target: To snare the hottest new resort business in Las Vegas, many casinos are building more convention and meeting space. *Casino Journal*, 12(7), 56–58.

5. Palermo, D. (2002, October). Always evolving: The Strip promises to change over the next few years. *International Gaming and Wagering Business*, 23(10), 1–35.

6. Ross, J. R. (2000, May). Gaming destination growth remains on upward spiral. *Convene*, XV(4), 74.

7. Nigro, D. (1998, June). Betting on meetings. *Meetings & Conventions*, 33(7), 60.

8. Finney, M. I. (1997, March). High stakes relationships: Casinos and conventions. *Association Management*, 49(3), 64–66.

9. Cook, M. (2000, June). New in gaming. *Meetings & Conventions*, 36(7), 51–58.

10. Convention Industry Council (2004). *About CIC*. Retrieved October 10, 2007. Online at http://www.conventionindustry.org/aboutcic/about_cic.htm.

11. Convention Industry Council (2005). *APEX industry glossary*. Retrieved October 30, 2007. Online at http://www.conventionindustry.org/apex/apex.htm. "Meeting."

12. Berns, D. (2001, April). Mandalay Bay: Casino to add convention space. *Las Vegas Review Journal*, 1D.

13. Ibid.

14. Smith, R. (2003, October). Earnings climb for Venetian parent: Convention business helps buoy result analyst says. *Las Vegas Review Journal*, Website: 1.

15. Berns, D. (2001, April). Mandalay Bay: Casino to add convention space. *Las Vegas Review Journal*, 1D.

16. Macy, R. (2000, February). Casino Executive: Vegas just scratching the surface in convention business. *Associated Press State and Local Wire*: http://Lexis-nexis.com.

17. Grimaldi, L. (2000, September). Atlantic City's gamble. *Meetings & Conventions*, 35(7), 87–90.
18. (Ghitelman, 1997:79).
19. Nigro, D. (1998, June). Betting on meetings. *Meetings & Conventions*, 33(7), 60.
20. Grimaldi, L. (2000, September). Atlantic City's gamble. *Meetings & Conventions*, 35(7), 87–90.
21. Heilman, J. (2006, December/January). *Meetings East*.
22. (Ghitelman, 1997:80).
23. Nigro, D. (1998, June). Betting on meetings. *Meetings & Conventions*, 33(7), 60.
24. Plume, J. (2001, May). Not by gaming alone. *Casino Journal*, XIV(5), 42–44.
25. Nigro, D. (1998, June). Betting on meetings. *Meetings & Conventions*, 33(7), 60.
26. Harris, E. (2000, April). Going native. *Successful Meetings*, 89–91.
27. Ibid.

CHAPTER 6

SEGMENTATION AND POSITIONING

KATHRYN HASHIMOTO

Learning Objectives

1. To provide an overview of the different types of marketing segmentation that casinos use
2. To understand the use of geographic segmentation in casino marketing
3. To understand the use of demographic segmentation in casino marketing
4. To understand the use of psychographic segmentation in casino marketing
5. To understand the use of behavioral segmentation in casino marketing
6. To learn the requirements for effective segmentation in casino marketing
7. To learn about the importance of market positioning in the casino industry

Chapter Outline

INTRODUCTION

So far, we have discussed strategic planning, the external environments, and the consumer and organizational behaviors that affect casino decisions for the future. In this chapter, we will discuss the process of deciding how casinos divide up their guests into more manageable groups. In market segmentation, we will look at geographic, demographic, psychographic, and behavioral ways to assess what markets are most attainable for a casino. We explore some of the requirements for effective segmentation strategies. Once a casino understands what segments are already coming as well as the potential segments that might come, it can then develop target markets. This process is used to evaluate each segment to decide which group would be best for a casino to attract. From this, a casino can choose a market coverage strategy to reach those groups of people.

MARKET SEGMENTATION

Geographic Segmentation

With **geographic segmentation**, marketers divide their guests by the state, zip code, or country where they live. For example, before California approved Indian gaming, Las Vegas drew heavily from the state of California. As a result, there were great deals for the drive-in traffic. In Los Angeles, some of the casinos actually had buses that stopped at specific locations to pick up gamblers, took them to the casinos to play all night, and then brought them back home at dawn for free. This made sense because most gamblers played during the daytime and the casinos were less crowded at night. To fill the casino at night, marketers made it easy for people who work day time shifts to take a free bus to Las Vegas.

FIGURE 6.1 Airports enable tourists to come from outside the area to spend their money. This allows an infusion of fresh money into the local economy.

Source: Mark Edwards/Peter Arnold, Inc.

Many casinos divide their guests into tourists (people from outside the area) and locals (people who live nearby). Tourists are good for Las Vegas and Atlantic City because people can fly/drive in and spend a week or weekend at these destination locations. Generating more tourist visits means that money from outside the community is spent on local businesses. This is good because the community can use outside money for infrastructure, and taxable revenues are generated from outsiders. In order to assess the economic impact of tourists, research has focused on how much tourists spend and what they spend their dollars on. **Volume segmentation** is a process that has adopted the usage-rate segmentation and grouped travel markets based on either the length of stay or the volume of trip expenditures. In assessing the changes in target markets, it is important to look back at the different behavioral patterns in the volume segmentation of gamblers.

Historians have suggested that Las Vegas was originally built so that people in California would have an adult playground where they could do whatever they wanted, but not in their hometown so as not to jeopardize their reputations or families. While that has not been a popular theory in Las Vegas, it would now be supported by the slogan, "What happens in Vegas, stays in Vegas." Since Las Vegas is surrounded by desert, people had to drive a long distance to get there, which meant that in the early days of casinos, it was assumed that the most important gamblers would be from outside the normal commuting distance. Tourists brought outside money and bolstered the local economy.

While some drove to and from Las Vegas in a day, the majority of gamblers spent at least one night in the hotels. As Las Vegas became the Mecca of gambling, it drew tourists who expanded their plans to include spending their weekends and holidays there. As the competitive environment from riverboats and Native American casinos grew, Las Vegas expanded beyond casinos to become an entertainment destination in order to keep tourists coming. Attractions of internationally recognized entertainers, museums, Broadway-like productions and, of course, shopping areas such as Caesars Forum and Desert Passage created new reasons to come to Las Vegas. As a result, gamblers and nongamblers alike went to Vegas to spend their weekends and vacations.

Mouffakkir, et al.[1] have taken volume-usage principles and expanded them to test the myth that gamblers spend money only in the casinos and not in the community. According to their research, heavy spenders had higher expenditure levels for nongaming products than the light and medium buyers. However, this varied in terms of age and household income. Overall, the heavy spenders were younger, more affluent, and first-time visitors on their own, not on charters. In fact, their expenditures accounted for over 90% of the total spending by the three segments. These findings reinforce the trend for casinos to seek younger, more affluent gamblers by designing youthful entertainment venues and redesigning the bars to reflect a younger fashion taste. However, the question has been, does this 20–30-year-old market have enough money and numbers to be a viable segment?

As casinos spread beyond Las Vegas to Atlantic City, a different tourist segment has emerged. Atlantic City is situated perfectly within a three-hour commute to the most densely populated area of America between Philadelphia and New York City. In addition, it is within four to six hours of Boston and Washington, DC. As a result, Atlantic City developed the fine art of bussing guests to its location. For a relatively inexpensive fee, people could board a bus that had food, beverages, and video entertainment, and could relax until they got to the casino. As the buses picked up people from farther and farther

FIGURE 6.2 Usually there is a special bus entrance in the casino complex for guests to meet their buses.

away, people could sleep on the bus before and after their activities. However, Atlantic City was also a place where people could drive to and play. In the 1980s, gamblers had a choice of 12 casinos to drive to for dinner, a show, some gambling, and then leave. This was the beginning of the local market as a viable market segment.

Researchers have found that tourists tended to have higher educational levels, were more likely to have jobs in management/professional areas, and were more motivated by the social environment of casinos. On the other hand, local patrons tended to be motivated by the excitement associated with the risks or rush of gambling. The smaller casino operations outside the two major gambling cities were not able to draw enough tourists to their sites because they did not have the synergistic effect of Las Vegas, nor did they have an easily accessible casino, like Atlantic City, where large numbers of visitors could come. Therefore, as riverboats and Native American casinos grew in numbers, they looked more toward local patrons.

As a rule, people do not fly in to these local casinos to gamble. The local clientele live within easy, short drives from the casino. As a result, they can play any day of the week for short periods of time. The phrase "**local market**" was invented in Las Vegas to address the neighborhood casinos that had grown to be a large and dynamic part of the total number of gamblers. Locals are defined as "driving-distance" gamblers who usually can gamble and go out for evening recreation during the week.

Local markets are different from tourist markets. Because of the frequent visits, the venue must be constantly changing so that people do not become bored. Gambling is an important part of the entertainment, but there must be more to keep people coming back. Local casinos need key features such as locations near major thoroughfares for easy access and plentiful parking with transportation that takes people right to the door. In addition, there must be other attractions such as dining, movie theaters, live entertainment, and

FIGURE 6.3 A large parking lot with transportation to the entrance of the casino is a must for locals.

childcare. A special segment within this market is the senior set. While we will talk about these people as a special group, it is important to add touches such as VIP clubs for seniors. In other words, you must have a total entertainment facility to keep the people coming back night after night. "The way I look at it, if I lose one customer, it's like losing 50 customers, because that customer is here 50 times a year,"[2] says George Maloof, Jr., Fiesta Casino Hotel president.

Shoemaker and Zemke[3] studied the "local" markets because they suggested that there were relatively little empirical data on this segment. Their study identified reasons why people would visit a particular casino, how they decided their gambling budget, their length of time gambling, and their favorite games. As gambling growth exploded, Steve Wynn, a prominent casino developer, convinced people that "gambling is only another form of recreation."

According to this argument, locals have a choice of how they spend their recreation budget. They can go to the movies, out to dinner, bowling, or to a casino on Saturday night. Going to a casino was no longer a major decision such as where to spend the weekend or a vacation. It was a simple alternative to other activities available in the area. While previous tourist research focused on economic impact and destination attractiveness, recent research on locals began to explore how often gamblers visited casinos and how they spent their money. In addition, it was found that friends and family had a decided effect on the frequency of repeat visitors. When friends and family visited a casino, 65.8% of the sample said they would accompany them to the casino if they went. In fact, 17% of locals would go to casinos only when hosting visitors.[4] From the broad distinction between tourists and local gamblers of the geographic segmentation, the other segmentation processes can be divided into demographic, psychographic, and behavioral segmentation.

Demographic Segmentation

Demographic segmentation relates to objective statistical information about an individual. Therefore, a casino can create a demographic profile that includes data such as age, family life cycle, income, race, gender, and educational level. For example, earlier we discussed that young adults who are less than 35 years of age are a new potential segmentation for casinos. However, they often do not have the disposable income of their elders, and there are more demands on their money. From this point, we see that demographic variables really do not give us a clear picture of who these people are. Therefore, we first create a demographic profile, but then immediately add psychological information about these people.

Psychographic Segmentation

Psychographic segmentation looks at activities, interests, and opinions of the people we have statistical information on. So, for our young adults under 35 years of age, we can add that these young adults look for where they can get the most entertainment for the dollars they have. Therefore, casinos trying to attract this group offer amenities such as microbreweries, themed venues offering nightly entertainment, brick-oven pizzas, oversized hamburgers, and large appetizers. While attempting to create an entire recreational package, it is also important for casinos to have multiple wide-screen monitors for sporting events. However, since many in the 20–30-year-old group have young children (family life cycle), on-premise childcare and other family-oriented, nongaming activities aid in drawing these young families to the casino. Traditional advertising methods such as radio, TV, and newspapers seem to bypass many younger people in this Internet-savvy age. More young adults get their news and information via the Internet. Younger gamblers like table games that provide the social interaction that they enjoy.[5] However, the question is

FIGURE 6.4 The 20–30-somethings enjoy socializing in the bars and gambling at the tables.

Source: Getty Images—Stockbite.

whether attracting these young people is worth the money spent. That is, do they have enough money to spend to balance out the cost of doing business with them? On the other hand, creating brand loyal guests now will assure the casino that they can have future clients for many years to come.

On the other hand, most of the local casinos have the Frank Sinatra–style entertainers for the seniors, and entertainers from the 1960s–1970s such as Credence Clearwater Revisited and Tina Turner for the baby boomers. Because the highest percentage of gamblers are seniors, many casinos have explored how to attract them. Hope and Havir[6] used **social exchange theory** to explain why seniors gamble. This theory explains social change and stability as a process of negotiated exchanges between parties. It suggests that all social relationships are perceived from the use of a subjective cost-benefit analysis and the comparison of alternatives. In this case, seniors derive pleasure out of their social interactions at the casino, and their experiences also give them a topic of conversation and shared rapport with all ages. Thus, it is a good trade-off for them between the money they spend and the interactions received.

On the other hand, Zaranek and Chapleski[7] used a Russian cultural-historical theory from the 1920s–1930s to analyze urban elders' desire to gamble. This theory, known as **activity theory**, suggests that the human mind can be analyzed only by understanding the context of meaningful, goal-oriented, and socially determined interactions between human beings and their material environment. The theory consists of a set of basic principles concerning how to develop a conceptual framework to study people's motivation in their lives and in their activities. In this case, gambling provides a meaningful, goal-oriented activity for urban elders. For example, in New York City, many elders are concerned about their safety when walking around the city and, thus, a bus trip to Atlantic City for a day gives them the freedom to walk around, enjoy the ocean, be with other seniors, and experience some excitement by gambling. In addition, gambling reinforces and enhances seniors' self-image. Therefore, besides gambling, a simple casino trip encompasses many factors that are desirable.

FIGURE 6.5   The largest gambling segment is seniors.

Source: Trish Gant © Dorling Kindersley.

Attracting seniors to gambling has become a social and political issue as younger people feel the need to protect their parents. For example, in New York City, politicians in the 1990s tried to block casino buses. The rationale was that seniors were not mentally capable of making those decisions because it was believed that they were becoming addicted and spending their life savings on going to Atlantic City to gamble. The very strong response to this action was that seniors were not senile and that they had budgeted their own money for longer than these politicians had been alive. They had lived through the Depression and, as a result, older people were quite capable of making their own decisions and managing their own money. Research from Stitt, Giacopassi, and Nichols[8] supported this viewpoint. Their results indicated that

> casino gambling is not a major threat to the elderly and it does not prey on the aged and lead them to destructive gambling practices . . . elderly, although visiting casinos more frequently than younger gamblers, generally exercise better money management and experience proportionately fewer gambling problems than the general population. (p. 199)

However, another problem with senior segmentation arose as Higgins[9] looked at the senior trips from a political framework. Many publically funded senior centers have developed field trips to different destinations, including casinos. Therefore, municipal funding is supplied by local and state tax dollars to develop, organize, and run these trips to the casinos. There are many people who still believe that gambling is not an ethical, moral, or religiously appropriate activity. Therefore, they believe that tax dollars should not be used to support any trips to a casino. However, this is a two-sided sword, since local and state governments are increasingly dependent on gambling and gambling-related tax revenue as a source of support for their programs, including senior centers. There is a dilemma as to whether senior centers should "support" casinos by planning and providing transportation for these trips using tax money even though the source of the tax money is the gambling venues. Therefore, even segmentation strategies need to be examined for unexpected complications in the macroenvironment.

As discussed earlier with young people under 35, family life cycle is another variable in segmentation. Typically a family life cycle is single status, to married, to full nest (with children), to empty nest (no children), to survivor (only one remaining). This sociological phenomenon was created in the 1950s when the nuclear family included two parents and two kids, preferably one boy and one girl. Now, however, as the family unit drastically changes with the times, it is much more difficult to assess. However, if we explore the difference in spending habits in recreation between a **DINK** (Double Income No Kids) couple with a couple who plans on children, we can see a quick example. If two people are planning on children, they will be more practical about their durable furniture and buying a house. Their entertainment and travel will be more conservative in preparation for expenses of having children and maybe their college education. On the other hand, DINK couples do not have to worry about budgeting for kids. Therefore, they can be more hedonistic in spending their entertainment budget because they have more discretionary income.

Many casinos realize that millions of potential customers are unable to afford long-distance travel for multinight vacations with quality childcare. However, many could plan shorter overnight stays, especially if their children could be supervised during these visits.

Kids Quest needs to be located conveniently for parents so that kids do not have to walk through the casino to get there. Casinos are now complete entertainment complexes that have all the amenities that resorts have. Typically, a Kids Quest center can handle 250 kids at a time or 1,000 per day at $12 per hour. The combined sites called "Kids Quest" (childcare) and "Cyber Quest" (amusement games) are supervised and secure, allowing parents the peace of mind to feel confident about their children's safety while enjoying the gaming floor. The Kids quest hourly childcare centers sit adjacent to the Cyber Quest arcades.[10]

As a result of the casino's desire to attract the demographic variable of families, an entrepreneur created a family entertainment venue so that parents could feel comfortable gambling knowing that their kids were having fun too.

Another demographic variable is ethnicity and/or country of origin. Many casinos have targeted local Asian Americans since there are usually a large number in the high-roller segment. In addition, many Asians travel to the United States to gamble and spend a lot of money. Many of the **whales** (people with gambling lines in excess of a million dollars) are from Asia. As a result, some casinos have targeted this segment. In fact, Harrah's even created an Asian training module so that its employees could learn some of the idiosyncrasies of the group. Typically, Asians are involved in civic events, and they maintain a high profile at various gatherings and dinners. Catering to their needs and wants shows proper respect for their position in life, which is an important cultural value. Therefore, making sure they are comfortable and developing the amenities they like will keep them coming back.

> When we were building our Asian games room, Paul Liu conceived the structure of four Chinese restaurants. Dynasty was a noodle bar in the pit to enable people to eat authentic Chinese soups and noodles. If it wasn't there, they might have to go down the street to eat and maybe they'd stay away. We also hired Chinese chefs to add Chinese menu items in both our 24-hour coffee shop and gourmet restaurant. Raymond Mui produces all Chinese shows that have been extremely successful. It took a lot of guidance and input when we were preparing to open the Asian games room. We had courses and seminars on the customers, habits, and tendencies of the Asian player. We try to sensitize pit personnel to some general cultural trends and superstitions and maybe teach them a few basic phrases. Being aware of the culture makes sense when you bring people in and you want them to come back.[11]

Throughout these examples, you will notice that casinos always begin by narrowing down the population with a demographic profile (for example, Asian, under 35, or seniors). Once casinos have a target market, they can begin to explore the psychological profile to see what the people like and how they think. A Harris Poll says, "74% of U.S. adults say they wish there were more products and services customized to their personal needs and tastes. In addition, 70% say they are more loyal to companies that make an effort to get to know what they want and 70% say they'd be willing to pay a premium for that attention."[12] These numbers make it worth our while to do the necessary research to understand our guests.

> The Silverton is unique in that we have a hotel and RV park. The 450 space KOA park brings us customers from around the world because we're on the

KOA Web site and KOA members can make their own reservations as they travel around the country. KOA also shares their database with us and this allows us to market directly to their members. Now these are people we want. They are retired or semi retired, have the time to travel and have discretionary income. When they do come here, they stay 2–3 weeks or longer and Silverton becomes their home where they play and eat. We invest in them and build a strong loyalty and that's what you need in this competitive environment.
—Scott Eldredge, Director of Marketing, Silverton Hotel & Casino[13]

Like in our example, Scott understands who his casino's clients are. He targets the demographic profile: retired or semi-retired and with or without discretionary income. Once he creates a simple profile, he researches their psychographics: can make their own reservations as they travel, want to travel, and stay two to three weeks or longer. In addition, he knows that they own campers and/or like to stay at KOA sites. From this evaluation of their wants and needs, he then creates a micromarketing plan to satisfy them. The product is a hotel and RV park, and the price is affordable to attract travelers who are traveling for a long period of time. They provide their own transportation, and they like to drive to different locations, so Silverton provides them with a place to park and entertainment while they stay. Promotions are advertising on the KOA Web site and direct marketing through the KOA database.

Behavioral Segmentation

In gaming, there appears to be no demographic profile that can be used to pinpoint exactly who will be a gambler. So, **behavioral segmentation** patterns can be used to give a clue as to who comes. For example, there are many people who come to Las Vegas in the summertime. They are in all income brackets, ages, family life cycles, and ethnicities, but they do have some behavioral patterns in common. It appears that with the high

FIGURE 6.6   The comfort of home while traveling the country.
Source: Clayton Sharrard/PhotoEdit Inc.

summer temperatures in the desert, more budget-minded tourists swap physical comfort for cheaper rooms and other concessions. As a result, they tend to avoid the expensive shows. Roy Jernigan, showroom producer, Orleans Hotel said, "Everybody should have learned a lesson from what happened (at the new year) when so many big shows failed to draw crowds because of the cost."[14] In addition, as casinos asked guests questions about their preferred form of entertainment, they found that not only were these clients more price conscious, they were often comfortable going to one show and they did not feel the need to go out every night. " 'I think they are going for quality over quantity these days,' says Chip Lightman, Danny Gans manager. 'They shop around more when trying to find the best entertainment experiences.' Richard Sturm, VP of worldwide entertainment for the MGM Grand says 'I think people already know what they want to see before they arrive. And if it's something they really want to see, they will buy a ticket.' "[15]

As we said, although there is a lot of research on tourists, there appears to be no demographic profile that can reliably identify who will be a gambler and who will not. As a result, one of the ways that casinos identify new players is through loyal, regular customers. For example, regular guests are often offered a cruise or party to which they can invite their 10 or 20 closest friends. When the new friends arrive, they are given player's club cards so that they can be given offers. The assumption is that people tend to have friends just like them, with the same values and interests. Therefore, if Joe likes to gamble a lot, he will probably have friends who might like gambling too. So, if we invite Joe's friends for a party or cruise, there is a higher likelihood that they will stay longer after the event and come more often with him in the beginning, but later by themselves. We have already learned that people who come with friends and family stay longer at casinos than people who come by themselves.

REQUIREMENTS FOR EFFECTIVE SEGMENTATION

As we explore the different types of segmentation that are available, some rules for effective segmentation should be in place. First, it is important for the segment to be measurable. Can you quantify how many people belong to this group? Do they have enough money to visit a casino and gamble? Second, how accessible are they? Can we reach them as a group easily? Is the group large enough? In the gaming industry sometimes one is a large enough group if he/she has a gambling line of $3 million. But for the most part, if casinos are trying to attract a group like the under-35 year olds that we discussed earlier, is the group large enough to warrant special attention? Finally, does the segment have enough requirements for the first three so that we could create an effective cost-effective program to attract them? Now of course this ability would depend on whether you want to attract tourists or locals. A casino in Las Vegas may not be interested targeting Greenville, North Carolina, but a casino attracting locals in North Carolina might be.

When casinos began offering bingo, no one thought to profile the players. Everyone "knew" the typical player was a grandmother, blue-tinted hair retiree between the ages of 63 and 67. However, as computerized games have infiltrated the industry, younger players of all ages, men and women, have been drawn to the bingo parlor. Now middle-aged to elderly women still are the largest demographic profile of bingo players, but the numbers of other players are also increasing.[16]

MARKET POSITIONING

When you select target markets and segment the population accordingly, you also need to think about how to position the casino to attract these guests. This includes designing the product, price, place, and promotions. For example, Mandalay Bay identified two distinct demographics that it wanted when the hotel opened. The first was the young, affluent adults who are successful at an early age. The second was the 45–55-year olds who are also well-to-do. In terms of the psychographics for these groups, both love life, like to have fun, enjoy themselves, and are social animals who like traveling and playing with their friends.[17] As a result, Mandalay Bay created a beautiful hotel with gorgeous rooms, fine restaurants, and an 11-acre pool area. In addition, for entertainment, there are the House of Blues, Shark Reef, and many special events that target its clientele.

> Look around the hotel, especially at our restaurants. The décor, food and atmosphere in Aureole, China Grill, 3950, Red Square, Lupo, and all the rest talk to these people who know where they are in life. They're comfortable with themselves and enjoy entertaining themselves and each other. We make it very easy for them to do all of this. It's the same with our entertainment. Billy Idol, The B-52s, the Three Tenors featuring Pavarotti, Heart, and Lynyrd Skynyrd are featured acts that match up well with our customer base. We have developed a niche market with different age groups but who are actually very compatible with each other. We send focused direct mail inviting them for various events and activities. But as I said, we have a hotel that is not just one thing. It's many exciting things and the people we're after know the Mandalay Bay is the place to be in Las Vegas.—John Marz, Senior VP of Marketing and Events, Mandalay Resort Group.[18]

Conclusion

Markets are groups of people who possess the purchasing power and the authority and willingness to buy your products. The role of market segmentation is to divide the total market into several groups. Each group's members are relatively homogeneous, with similar product interests. When we look at bases for market segmentation, some of the segments are geographic, demographic, psychographic, and behavioral. The advantages of creating segments is that it is easier to identify and evaluate opportunities in the marketplace, optimally allocate and direct resources, and tailor the marketing mix to the market. Keep in mind that fundamental marketing strategies dictate that only meaningful customer differences should delineate market segments and that the customer relationship should be perfectly managed against those segments. That said, "Consumer groups are getting cut into smaller and smaller segments as if more segments guarantee better results. Ultimately, too many segments yield only vague differences between customers."[19]

Key Words

Review Questions

1. Give an overview of the different types of marketing segmentation that casinos use.
2. Detail the uses of geographic segmentation in casino marketing.
3. Detail the uses of demographic segmentation in casino marketing.
4. Detail the uses of psychographic segmentation in casino marketing.
5. Detail the uses of behavioral segmentation in casino marketing.
6. Describe the requirements for effective segmentation in casino marketing.
7. Explain the importance of market positioning in the casino industry.

Endnotes

1. Moufakkir, O., Singh, A. J., Moufakkir-van der Woud, A., & Holecek, D.F. (2004). Impact of light, medium and heavy spenders on casino destinations: segmenting gaming visitors based on amount of non-gaming expenditures. *UNLV Gaming Research & Review Journal*, 8(1), 59–71.
2. Green, M. (2000). Local favorites. *IGWB*, 21(3), 1, 22.
3. Shinnar, R., Young, C., & Corsun, D. (2004). Las Vegas locals as gamblers and hosts to visiting friends and family: characteristics and gaming behavior. *UNLV Gaming Research & Review Journal*, 8(2), 39–48.
4. Ibid.
5. Burton, K. (2003). Pumping up the volume. *Global Gaming Business*, 2(9), 32–33.
6. Hope, J., & Havir, L. (2002). You bet they're having fun! Older Americans and casino gambling. *Journal of Aging Studies*, 16(2), 177–198.
7. Zaranek, R., & Chapleski, E. (2005). Casino gambling among urban elders: just another social activity? *Journals of Gerontology Series B: Psychological Sciences & Social Sciences*, 60B(2), S74–S81.
8. Stitt, B., Giacopassi, D., & Nichols, M. (2003). Gambling among older adults: a comparative analysis. *Experimental Aging Research*, 29(2), 189–203.
9. Higgins, J. (2005). Exploring the politics and policy surrounding senior center gambling activities. *Journal of Aging Studies*, 19(1), 85–107.
10. Harris, J. (2005). Kids Quest. *Global Gaming Business*, 5(4), 36.
11. Grochowski, J. (2000). An Eastern flavor. *IGWB*, 21(4), 23.
12. Fitzpatrick, M. (2004). Divide and conquer. *Casino Journal*, 17(11), 49.
13. Bulavsky, J. (2002). The marketing manifesto. *Casino Journal*, 15(9), 77.
14. Paskevich, M. (2000). Summer players shop for bargains. *IGWB*, 21(8), 3.
15. Ibid., 39.
16. Plume, J. (2002). Any number can play. *Casino Journal*, 15(3), 32–37.
17. Bulavsky, J. (2002). The marketing manifesto. *Casino Journal*, 15(9), 75–77.
18. Ibid.
19. Buro, F. (2006). Emotional rescue. *Casino Journal*, 19(1), 25.

PART TWO

Micromarketing
Things That a Casino Can Control

CHAPTER 7

APPLYING THE SERVICE-PROFIT CHAIN

DAVID C. WILLIAMS

Learning Objectives

1. To understand the concept of internal service quality
2. To learn the attributes that contribute to a firm's internal service quality
3. To learn the role of workplace design in internal service quality
4. To learn the role of job design in internal service quality
5. To learn the role of employee selection and development in internal service quality
6. To learn the role of employee rewards and recognition in internal service quality
7. To learn the role of tools for serving customers in internal service quality
8. To understand the role of employee satisfaction to the service-profit chain
9. To understand the role of employee retention to the service-profit chain
10. To understand the concept of external service quality
11. To learn the role of customer satisfaction in external service quality
12. To learn the role of customer loyalty in external service quality
13. To understand the role of profitability and revenue growth in the service-profit chain

Chapter Outline

INTRODUCTION

So far, we have discussed the macromarketing environments that affect the operations of a casino. We started by discussing how to create a strategic plan and how environmental scanning was the first step. From there we looked at the different external environments and how they can change how a casino plans for the future. Each of the environments impacts on the buyers, and on how they buy. Chapter 6 focused on segmenting these different groups into manageable sizes so that casinos can create marketing plans to attract each segment. Beginning with this chapter, we will explore how casinos use the information from the external environment in order to create effective micromarketing plans for their product, price, place, and promotions. This is, in other words, taking the factors we cannot control and deciding how we can use those ideas to create productive plans with factors that we can control.

In the other volumes of this series, we have discussed the tangible products of the casinos, such as the games, hotels, and restaurants. Therefore, rather than repeat the material, this chapter focuses on the most important aspect of a casino and its amenities: service.

Casinos are very similar in terms of products. Generally, they all have the same table games, mechanical games, bingo, and so on. In addition, many casinos have hotels, restaurants, and recreational activities. While we could spend some time discussing their outside themes or the interior designs that make guests feel more comfortable with the property, these are aspects that, if found successful, can be copied by the competitors. On the other hand, people are unique. If employees call me by my first name and they seem glad to see me, it makes me feel special. It also makes me seem important to anyone I bring with me to the casino. If I can call the dealers by their names and receive a smiling response, I feel more at home, more comfortable in my surroundings. Therefore, one of the most important factors in a successful visit is happy, motivated employees.

FIGURE 7.1 Happy employees interact with guests with smiles and help.

Source: Corbis Digital Stock.

In 1994, five professors, James H. Heskett, Gary W. Loveman, Thomas O. Jones, W. Earl Sasser, and Leonard A. Schlesinger from the Harvard Business School published an article called "Putting the Service-Profit Chain to Work" in the *Harvard Business Review*.[1] Three years later Heskett, Sasser, and Schlesinger followed this groundbreaking article with the book *The Service Profit Chain: How Leading Companies Link Profit and Growth to Loyalty, Satisfaction, and Value*.[2] Over the past decade, companies in industries ranging from banking and retail to hospitality and casinos have applied the tenets of the service-profit chain theory. The **service-profit chain** offers both elegant simplicity and commonsense application. To summarize, it simply suggests that happy, motivated employees create satisfied customers, which leads to increased profitability and revenue growth for your company.

Another way to summarize the service-profit chain is to suggest that:

Employee satisfaction → Customer satisfaction → Revenue growth.

First, an organization creates a culture where employees' needs are important which ensures that employees are happy. Second, happy employees are more motivated to go the extra mile to improve the guest's visit thereby satisfying the needs of customers better. Satisfied customers are more loyal, and so they are easier to retain. They come back more often and refer other customers. Finally, the increase in business levels leads to increased profitability and revenue growth. The beauty of the service-profit chain is that a portion of increased profits are reinvested in employee satisfaction that restarts the service-profit chain cycle.

Figure 7.1 shows a recreation of the service-profit chain as described in the *Harvard Business Review Article*: "Putting the Service-Profit Chain to Work."

Each box in Figure 7.1 is considered a link in the service-profit chain. By strengthening each link in the chain, a company can build loyalty among employees and customers in order to increase profitability. The rest of this chapter explains the service-profit chain link by link and offers a series of insights into applying the service-profit chain to a casino resort operating environment.

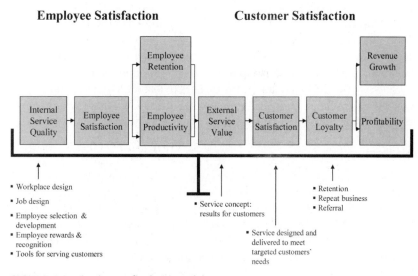

FIGURE 7.2 Service-profit chain model.

INTERNAL SERVICE QUALITY

The first link of the service-profit chain is the **internal service quality**. The concept of service quality is well researched in the realm of marketing business theory. *Service quality* is the term used to describe a service experience. When you purchase a durable good, such as a car, quality is defined by how well the item works. Guarantees such as a 100,000-mile warranty or no scheduled maintenance for the first three years speak to the quality of the car. But many services don't leave the customer with something tangible on which to judge quality. Therefore, the concept of service quality was developed to help organizations understand that a customer's feeling of satisfaction in a service experience can lead to similar perceptions of quality as that of buying a good.

Internal service quality takes the concept of service quality and applies it to the workplace. In an organization the final producers of a service are supported by a variety of other employees who make up the organization. For example, customers arrive at a restaurant because of marketing decisions made by a resort's marketing team. Forecasts for the number of employees needed to meet the level of customer demand come from the Finance department, and make it possible for the proper number of servers to staff the restaurant. From the perspective of the waitstaff, the chefs and stewards make it possible for the team of waiters to serve customers throughout the evening easily.

The authors of the *Service-Profit Chain* list five attributes that contribute to a firm's internal service quality. The factors are workplace design, job design, employee selection and development, employee rewards and recognition, and tools for serving customers. Each of these attributes can be identified in the casino resort workplace.

Workplace Design

Workplace design is evident in the layout of a casino. Casino slot floor design can help or hinder the job of a slot employee. Lines of sight that allow customers to see across the casino also help employees more easily identify customers in need of service. In an effort to improve workplace design, I ordered the new ergonomically designed dealer chairs for our poker dealers. However, it turned out that the dealers found the chairs uncomfortable to sit in for a full shift.

I immediately went to the dealers and explained my mistake. My heart was in the right place, as I had bought what were advertised as the most comfortable dealer chairs available, but I had not asked the dealers to test the chairs first. I then had several chair vendors deliver a variety of new dealer chairs for the dealers to test for a month. The end result is that I ate the cost of the first chairs and bought a new set of chairs overwhelmingly endorsed by the dealers. The moral here is that employees should be involved in workplace design decisions.

Job Design

Job design in a casino is always changing as new technologies change the customer experience. At the turn of the century most casino slots paid off with coins. While the sound of coins dropping in the slot machine tray was linked to the concept of excitement on the casino floor, the use of coins impacted the job design of a slot attendant. A central part of a slot attendant's job involved refilling slot machines with coins. This meant carrying 20- to 40-pound bags of coins from the casino cage to each slot machine.

With the introduction of TITO (Ticket In Ticket Out) systems, coins were eliminated from the casino floor. The removal of coins completely changed the job of a slot attendant.

In the past, the primary job requirement to a slot attendant was the ability to carry 20- to 40-pound bags of coins; now the job of a slot attendant is focused on customer service.

Employee Selection and Development

Employee selection and development is central to any organization. In a casino resort environment, selection is about choosing employees who like to interact with customers. A customer service focus is central to success and satisfaction for people working in a casino. Casinos are also known for promoting employees from within. By developing employee skills and growing employee careers, casino resorts help build internal service quality.

Employee Rewards and Recognition

Research in the areas of human and organizational behavior has demonstrated the positive impact that rewards and recognition have in the workplace. They offer feedback to all employees concerning which acts are valued by the organization. They tell the world that this person has traits that we want copied by all our employees. Sometimes all a person needs is a simple "thank you for a job well done." Employee of the month programs, team of the month programs, and individual recognition for acts of valor are additional examples of rewards and recognition in the casino resort workplace. Public recognition of a job well done can have a greater impact than some financial rewards. However, there are usually additional perks like closer parking spaces or time off for people who are motivated by other reasons.

Tools for Serving Customers

Tools for serving customers are central to an employee's daily job satisfaction. Quite often, we can find the right tools by allowing our employees to help us. Several years ago I took over the role of running an established casino operation. After meeting with employees

FIGURE 7.3 Public recognition for a job well done helps motivate people to continue the good job they are doing.

Source: Dorling Kindersley.

from several departments, it became clear that a common theme of dissatisfaction was our two-way radio system. Employees on the casino floor needed to be in constant contact with employees across a variety of departments, and our system had a habit of cutting out or filling the airwaves with static. We created a task force of employees who used the radios, to investigate a new radio system. The task force found that our radios were fine; the issue was in the radio signal repeater system. After purchasing a series of radio signal repeaters, we resolved the issue and employees across all of the casino departments had the tools they needed to better serve our guests.

Employee Satisfaction

Internal service quality is used to increase employee satisfaction. Just as satisfied customers are more likely to be repeat customers, satisfied employees are more likely to remain with a company. Happy employees results in less time off and less turnover. People tend to stay with a company when they like working there. The results are less money spent on recruitment and training for the company. This is important for the profit margin. The service-profit chain suggests that employee satisfaction is as important as customer satisfaction.

While many organizations measure customer satisfaction, the concept of surveying employee satisfaction is not as widespread. As with customer satisfaction, the only way to know if employees are satisfied is to ask them. Whether this is done with employee focus groups, an annual survey, or with **MBWA** (managing by walking around), employee satisfaction should not be overlooked.

I cannot overstate the importance of employee satisfaction. Frontline employees are your link to the customer. If you are providing a service, your frontline employees are the service providers. How they treat your customers is based upon how they feel about your organization.

In September 2001, the casino I was running was impacted by the attack on the Twin Towers in New York. Customers stopped traveling for several months and our business tanked. As business levels plummeted, it became clear that we needed to layoff a number of employees. The drop in business levels was seen immediately by our employees, and they all knew layoffs were coming.

First, the layoffs became a major topic on the casino floor and the discussions of what might take place happened between employees. Next, the discussion of impending layoffs started between our employees and our customers. Soon our customers were calling me to lobby for the jobs of their favorite employees. We should have acted more quickly to minimize the impact of discussion between our employees and our customers. The point is that your employees are your lifeline to your customers and when your employees are not satisfied, your customers will be the first to know about it.

Employee Retention

I have been told by a variety of human resource professionals that it costs between $3,000 and $5,000 to hire and train a new employee. The cost to hire and train a new employee is reason enough to focus on employee retention. However, in your casino resort long-term employees are central to your customers' experience. Your best customers spend a lot of time playing on your casino floor. With each jackpot or each time they sit at a table game, your customers interact with your employees. Over time, customers will get to know your employees and this relationship will play a role in keeping your customer coming back. In this way, employee retention ties directly to customer satisfaction.

Geoff Andres, a fantastic general manager I had the good fortune of working for, lived by the axiom that, "People don't quit a job, they quit a supervisor." Over the years I have found this to be true. In a slot department that I once ran, I found that turnover was close to zero, while turnover at our competitors was closer to the industry average of 30%. In my weekly meetings with frontline employees from this department I consistently heard about how the frontline employees felt their supervisors cared about them. It was the close relationship between employee and supervisor that created a comfortable workplace and enhanced employee satisfaction.

Employee Productivity

A second area impacted by employee satisfaction is employee productivity. The idea is that satisfied employees are more productive employees. While research on employee satisfaction and the link to employee productivity is mixed, the idea that the elements of internal service quality could improve productivity makes common sense. If employees have the tools to serve customers, the workplace is well designed, and the job is well designed to service customers, then employees will be able to offer higher levels of productivity than in a work environment with missing work tools, poor workplace design, or poor job design.

One well managed casino created a "employee concierge" position. Everyone knows that a concierge is someone who help guests with their problems. In this case, the employee concierge did the same thing. Employees could bring in their dry cleaning and the concierge would take it with the guest's items to be cleaned. Bank transactions or pharmacy pickups or even small grocery orders could be handled by the concierge. At first glance, it would appear to be a luxury for the employees. However, think about it. An employee probably spends an hour or more planning how they are going to get their errands done during their lunch hour. Then they have to eat lunch at their desk so that they have time for everything. With an employee concierge, it is a question of dropping off required items and picking everything up after shift. This saves the company the hour of planning and the time to eat lunch at their desk. This gives back to the company a couple of hours of productive work time. In addition, employees have a chance to relax during their lunch hour so that they come back ready to work.

Several years ago I worked with a slot department that had just introduced a TITO technology. The new technology changed every job in the department. Slot attendants, who were used to filling slot machines with coins all day, were now wondering what to do with their "free" time. Working with the management team, we developed a new service process that gave frontline employees a new tool to help them interact with customers. The problem was that employees used to talk to players as they filled empty slot machines with coins and now they needed a new tool to help kick-start the conversation. With this new tool, the slot attendants started interacting with more customers. Customer letters pointing out our great slot service poured into the general manager's office.

EXTERNAL SERVICE QUALITY

The concepts of internal service quality, employee satisfaction, employee retention, and employee productivity culminate in the customer experience, defined as **external service value** by the service-profit chain. Think of external service value as the service concept or the results for a customer. In the world of tax accounting the external service value could be measured by the tax refund you receive or the IRS (Internal Revenue Service) audit you avoid.

In a casino resort the concept of external service value can take on many shapes and forms, such as the feeling you have at the end of a wonderful meal, or the satisfaction you have after winning the weekly blackjack tournament, or the warm feeling you have from having spent a few hours matching wits with your opponents at the poker table, or staying up late enough to watch the sun rise over Las Vegas. These are just a few of the experiences that comprise external service value.

Customer Satisfaction

The service-profit chain links external service value to customer satisfaction. Customer satisfaction is central on the three key links, showing that

Employee satisfaction → Customer satisfaction → Revenue growth

Customer satisfaction represents an entire discipline of study in some business schools. A quick search of your business library will turn up multiple books on customer satisfaction and a plethora of research articles on the topic. In a world of increasing global competition, companies have found that finding what keeps customers satisfied is central to survival. When a customer has a variety of choices for either a service or a product, then the competing businesses must compete on either quality or price. In a service industry such as the casino industry, quality revolves around the service.

Customer satisfaction is what brought me to the casino industry early in my career. I was hired by a hotel casino company because of my expertise in developing customer satisfaction surveys for the service industry. After refining customer satisfaction surveys for several hotel chains, I had the opportunity to help develop the first customer satisfaction survey for the gaming industry. Many industry colleagues said that casino players could not be satisfied because most of them left the casino experience after losing money. Over the years, this logic has proven untrue. Casino players view their visits to a casino as a service experience. The vast majority of customers realize that the games they play are a form of entertainment and that the casino offers the games because of the house advantage. One customer put it best by saying, "there's a reason they (the casino) have the big building."

Customer satisfaction is central to the casino experience. When all casinos offer the same games, be it blackjack, video poker, slots, or keno, casino operators realize they are offering a commodity. If you are selling a commodity, then all you have to differentiate on is service. The need to differentiate your casino from the competition is why the service-profit chain applies so easily to the casino industry.

Customer Loyalty

The ultimate goal of creating satisfied customers is to drive customer loyalty. The casino industry is a repeat-business industry. People who like to gamble choose to visit casinos as their preferred form of entertainment. Golfers like to golf, movie buffs go to the movie theater, and gamblers visit casinos. The goal of a casino marketing program is to have gamblers choose its casino over their competitors' casinos. Like any other target market, there are a number of casinos competing for this limited supply of customers. The easiest

FIGURE 7.4 Motivated, satisfied employees can make happy customers as well as wins.

Source: Luc Beziat/Getty Images—Stone Allstock.

way to achieve the marketing goal of attracting gamblers is to attract many of the same gamblers each time they decide to visit a casino. You want to be the casino of choice among your target segment of casino players.

The service-profit chain points out three benefits an organization receives through building customer loyalty. Those benefits are retention, repeat business, and referral.

Retention points to the length of time a player stays at a casino. Casinos measure customer value based on the size of bet, the hold percentage of the game, and the length of play. These three variables are used to calculate theoretical player win by Table Games departments throughout the world.

The size of bet is straight forward. If the player is betting $5,000 per hand, then the player will be more valuable than a player betting $5 per hand. Hold percentage is simply the house edge over the play on any of the games of chance offered by the casino. For example, roulette has a hold percentage of 5.26%, which means that out of 20 spins of the roulette wheel the casino will win on 11 spins and the player will win on 9 spins. Retention is about length of play. The longer a player plays, the more he/she is worth to the casino.

Repeat business is different from retention in that repeat business involves the player making a decision to return to the casino. This is what many marketing plans are shooting for. When a player decides to visit a casino, the goal is that the player chooses your casino.

Referral is when a customer recommends a casino establishment to a friend or acquaintance. Referrals are new customers that a casino did not have to spend lots of marketing dollars to attract. This is the value of customer loyalty in the service-profit chain. The casino builds a base of players through positive word of mouth from current players.

In the service-profit chain, customer loyalty leads to customer retention, repeat business, and referrals. Each of these attributes means more customers play at a casino, and more players mean more money. Higher business levels should lead to higher profits, which brings us to the final two links in the service-profit chain: revenue growth and profitability.

Revenue Growth

The goal of a business is to make money. The service-profit chain suggests that if employees are satisfied, they will do a better job of satisfying customers. Satisfied customers are easier to retain as customers, more likely to offer repeat business, and more likely to refer friends as new customers. More customers increase the ability of a firm to grow revenues. A simple equation says that more customers = higher revenues. While a number of factors such as the value of each customer make this equation an over simplification, the basic concept should make sense. If casinos are able to attract more customers, then their revenues should grow.

Revenue is simply the funds that a company receives from customers when it sells a product or a service. In the case of a casino resort, revenues come from bets placed, restaurant meals served, hotel rooms sold, drinks consumed at the nightclubs, and so on. By building customer loyalty, a casino can grow revenue.

Profitability

Profitability is a second link in the Service-Profit Chain. Profitability is similar to revenue growth, but speaks to a company's ability to bring money to the bottom line. While a company may see increases in revenue, many companies find that to achieve higher revenues they must spend more and more money. This means that companies can find that they spend more to attract a customer than they can make from that customer. One of my favorite business fallacies is the saying, "What we lose on a per item basis, we make up for in volume." The fallacy of this statement is obvious because you cannot make money selling more of something if you lose money on each transaction. An example of this is a restaurant manager who decided to enter a highly competitive lunch buffet market by offering a seafood line of products for $9.99. From the first, his buffet was a huge success. There was a waiting line out the door every day at noon. After two months, he started to calculate the expense for the buffet versus the income. He found that if he paid every customer $2 to *not* eat at his buffet, he would break even. Many companies find themselves chasing new customers who ultimately end up unprofitable.

The final link in the service-profit chain points to how the model offers a means of creating a profitable business. Having loyal customers means that a company should spend less marketing dollars attracting those customers and by spending less marketing dollars the company should become more profitable. The two final links show a business leader how the service-profit chain can link employee satisfaction and customer satisfaction to a business' ultimate goals of revenue growth and profitability.

Conclusion

The service-profit chain is a model of business operation. The service-profit chain simply states that satisfied employees lead to satisfied customers, which will increase a firm's revenue and profitability. If a company focuses on keeping employees satisfied, the end result will be a more profitable company.

The following points offer an overview of key ideas from this chapter on the service-profit chain.

- Internal service quality drives employee satisfaction.
- Employee satisfaction leads to increased employee retention and productivity.

- External service value is what a casino offers customers.
- Customer satisfaction is driven by external service value.
- The goal of customer satisfaction is customer loyalty because customer loyalty includes retention, repeat business, and referral.
- Increased customer loyalty leads to revenue growth and profitability.

Key Words

Service-profit chain *87*
Internal service quality *88*
MBWA *90*

External service value *91*
Retention *93*

Repeat business *93*
Referral *93*

Review Questions

1. Define the concept of internal service quality.
2. Explain the role of workplace design in internal service quality.
3. Explain the attributes that contribute to a firm's internal service quality.
4. Discuss the role of job design in internal service quality.
5. Discuss the role of employee selection and development in internal service quality.
6. Explain the role of tools for serving customers in internal service quality.
7. Explain the role of employee satisfaction to the service-profit chain.
8. Discuss the role of employee retention to the service-profit chain.
9. Discuss the concept of external service quality.
10. Explain the role of customer satisfaction in external service quality.
11. Explain the role of customer loyalty in external service quality.
12. Discuss the role of profitability in the service-profit chain.

Endnotes

1. Heskett, J. L., Jones, T. O., Loveman, G. W., Sasser, Jr., W. E., and Schlesinger, L. A. (1994). Putting the service-profit chain to work. *Harvard Business Review*, March/April, 164–174.

2. Heskett, J. L., Sasser, Jr., W. E., and Schlesinger, L. A. (1997). *The Service Profit Chain: How Leading Companies Link Profit and Growth to Loyalty, Satisfaction, and Value.* New York: Free Press.

CHAPTER 8

REVENUE MANAGEMENT

KATHRYN HASHIMOTO

Learning Objectives

1. To become familiar with early pricing strategies of casinos
2. To become familiar with contemporary pricing strategies of casinos
3. To learn about the many aspects of defining revenue management
4. To learn about the eight ways of applying revenue management
5. To understand the importance of revenue management systems
6. To understand how revenue management systems apply to casino operations
7. To learn the ways of identifying profitable guests
8. To understand the levels of success of various revenue management systems
9. To learn about the cultural shift in thinking

Chapter Outline

Introduction
Early Pricing Strategies
Contemporary Pricing Strategies
Defining Revenue Management
Applying Revenue Management
Importance of Revenue Management
    Systems

How Do Revenue Management Systems
    Apply in Casinos?
Identifying Profitable Guests
How Successful are the Revenue
    Management Systems?
Cultural Shift in Thinking
Conclusion

INTRODUCTION

Since the beginning of time, man evaluated his possessions and attached some value to them. When other people agreed that his possessions did indeed have some value, they bartered to trade. Trade was based on **supply and demand** for each item. Like today, items that were scarce but desirable were worth more than items that were plentiful. In order to sell all the goods in his cart, a vendor had to decide which of his items were more valuable and therefore could command a higher "price." In this way, all of the items could be sold and the merchant could make the most profit.

EARLY PRICING STRATEGIES

This decision of using availability based on the supply and demand for each item to set price was the earliest form of revenue management. Using this principle of maximizing revenue, innkeepers would do the same. When the inn did not have any guests because it was a slow season, the price for the rooms could be set lower. However, as more people filled the inn and there were fewer rooms available, the price could be set higher. The supply of rooms was smaller; therefore, the demand should become greater. On the other hand, one had to be careful. If the price was set too high, travelers would seek shelter elsewhere and the innkeeper would have several rooms still available when it was too late to sell them. It was a decision involving one's best guess and judgment.

Another example of early pricing strategy was voyaging by ship or an early version of today's cruising industry. When the Titanic set sail, the best rooms (those at the top of the vessel) were sold at a high price to the wealthy so that they could enjoy the evening breezes and the salty air. As a result, the rooms were decorated very elaborately and sized to accommodate many trunks of clothes. On the other hand, the hold, which was dank, dark, and underwater, was reserved for the poor. Thus, those rooms were cramped and crowded, but the price was set low enough so that people without a lot of money could sail. In this way, every bit of space could be sold, and revenues were maximized.

In the food and beverage (**F&B**) industry, restaurants also used a form of pricing strategy for their foods. The noblemen received the best cuts of meat and the best ale because they could pay the most. The lesser cuts and the dregs of the beer barrel were sold cheaply so that nothing would be wasted. As the world changed and transportation evolved to include air travel, guests could sit in a plane and pay different prices based on their seat location. The front of the plane is often reserved for first-class guests who pay the most money for their seats. This can be two or three times more than coach seats. As a result, the airlines cater to these people with food and drink. That is because everyone likes to be in the front of the plane and be the first on and off, and many believe that the front is safer if the plane should have a mishap.

With the Airline Deregulation Act of 1978, airlines were able to compete with one another for passengers, fares, and routes. This resulted in price wars, which were good for passengers, but created budget problems for the airlines. As a result, the airlines developed a formalized method for managing and controlling revenues called **yield management**. *Yield* was the amount of revenue from each passenger mile. Another crucial factor for the airlines was the **load factor** that referred to the percentage of seats sold. With these two factors, the airlines began to statistically calculate the most profitable balance for each route. Keep in mind that there were many major airlines as well as smaller airlines all

FIGURE 8.1 Developing a pricing strategy with only a paper and pencil is a difficult process.

Source: Images.com.

competing for similar routes. It is always assumed that lower prices generate more purchases, so the first pricing strategy was to lower the price of the fares. The larger airlines offered lower prices to match the smaller airlines, and more seats on each plane at that rate. As a result, profits dropped. The lower prices meant less profit per passenger mile, even though the load factor (seats sold) was higher because it cost more for each trip because of more baggage, baggage handling, food and drink costs, more fuel, and ticketing.

So, the next attempt at pricing strategy was higher prices, which meant that the yield was higher per passenger mile, but the load factor was lower. Unfortunately, there are fixed costs with each trip. Therefore, there were not enough passengers paying a premium price to break even. Finally, during the 1980s, American Airlines decided to use their Sabre reservation system to calculate the proper yield management ratio between load and yield. They knew some of the demographics of their passengers and the fares these travelers would pay. For example, business passengers would pay more than leisure travelers who might seek more discounted prices. This allowed them to calculate the percentage of the passengers with certain characteristics for each flight for each day of the week. This data allowed them to create a value for each seat on each flight. This was the start of pricing strategies that included looking at revenue generated from each passenger mile.

CONTEMPORARY PRICING STRATEGIES

Once they started to analyze this data, companies realized that they needed an extra factor, booking pace, which showed the preflight booking patterns. When did people book their flights? Leisure passengers tended to book flights early, whereas business travelers were more likely to book late as their business needs demanded. As with most products that have a captured audience, people expect to pay higher prices when they buy at the last minute. Think about it. What is the price of beer at a ball game when you can't bring any beverages? Higher or lower than when you can bring in beverages? As a result, there is a small gap between the time the leisure travelers want their low prices and the business travelers enter the equation. Understanding those time frames allows airlines to offer cheaper prices early to assure full flights, but then increase prices at the last minute. The critical factor is knowing when to make the change. Fares were assigned to the different levels of seating with restrictions, in order to maximize revenue for each flight.

Then of course, the final step in any strategic plan is tracking the results and fine-tuning the plan. This requires looking at the current patterns of progress and comparing them to historical data for the same day and week over the years. It is always important to run these analyses thoughtfully. For example, whether December 25 falls on a Monday, a Friday, or on a weekend can change the purchase patterns. Many people like to take off the day before and after a holiday. If Christmas is on a Wednesday, they might be tempted to take the week off, which means flying the Friday before and staying until the Sunday after. On the other hand, if the Christmas holiday is a Monday then people might fly Saturday and come home Tuesday. By the same token, if May 5 was a Tuesday last year it would not be comparable to a Saturday this year. So, these comparisons need to be thought out and not just arbitrarily compared by using only a specific date every year.

As airlines began to turn around their profits, other hospitality enterprises began to assess whether this same system could work for them. However, unlike the airlines, few hotels had been keeping track of their guests in terms of who they were or why they were there. In addition, the hotels did not know when their guests actually booked the rooms. Therefore, there were very few data points on which to begin organizing historical data on guests. In addition, the yield management system from the airlines did not take into consideration the length-of-time factor of hotels. That is, airlines have a set time frame when people used their seats. Hotels do not. People can stay one night or multiple nights. Therefore, the airline system had to be adapted.

DEFINING REVENUE MANAGEMENT

Bill Marriott is often credited with being the pioneering force for initially championing revenue management in the hotel industry. The Marriott organization researched customer demand for their various hotel products. Based upon their findings, they determined that customer behavior and demand could be forecasted. If this was the case, then price levels and inventory controls could be established based upon the predicted demand each day. In other words, based on this forecast, Marriott could decide which rooms would be offered at which price for each day. Applying this technique to all hotels within their organization yielded Marriott an additional $100 million in yearly revenue in the first few years of implementation.[1]

When creating this new model for revenue control, planners were concerned about the availability of their product and what price they should charge. Therefore, the model included factors for capacity, supply, and demand. *Capacity* refers to the number of guests that the facility can handle or the amount of space to be filled. With hotels, capacity is the maximum number of rooms to be filled. With restaurants, it is the maximum number of seats in the dining rooms. This is also carefully regulated by public ordinances; you can

FIGURE 8.2 Putting heads in beds for the best profit is a difficult task.

see signs in public spaces designating the capacity of an elevator or a restaurant. This created a quantifiable definition for availability of the product. *Supply* is an economic term referring to the amount of goods and services that the facility is willing to sell. And, on the other side of the equation is the *demand*, or the amount of goods and services that a guest is willing and able to buy.

To create demand, Kemmons Wilson, founder of the Holiday Inn, trained all of his front-desk agents to ask departing guests where they were going after they left. Then, if the guests were still going to be away from home, the agent would then ask, "would you like me to make another reservation at the Holiday Inn at your next stop?" In this way, travelers could be assured of their next room for the night with a minimum amount of hassle, and a Holiday Inn would be assured of another night's stay.

In Scotland, all of the tourist information centers have a reservation service for bed and breakfasts (**B&B**). While B&Bs can be wonderful relaxing places similar to home, you might wonder whether one is safe and what the place is really like. This concern restricts many people from booking B&Bs. In Scotland, all the agents have visited the surrounding B&Bs and can give personal accounts of the innkeepers and their establishments. Therefore, it is easier to match the wants and demands of the traveler with the product and pricing of the B&B. This is reassuring to travelers and they are more likely to try someplace new.

We once deviated from the tourist information centers when we couldn't find a place to stay in the location we wanted to go. We pulled out our book on B&Bs and selected one. When we got there, the place was dark and the innkeeper's undergarments were hanging all over the front foyer. As we mounted the stairs to our room, we had visions of being mugged in the night. We were being stupid and immediately went out to dinner and had a lot of drinks to calm our nerves. However, the more drinks we had, the more nervous we got. Therefore, we went back, picked up our bags, and found the nearest commercial hotel. After that, we never strayed from the comforting tourist information centers and we were never disappointed again. The tourist information centers know the capacity for locations and offer suggestions based on the supply and projected demand.

Now that we have discussed the three major components (capacity, supply, and demand) of revenue management, the definition for revenue management is, "the act of skillfully, carefully, and tactfully managing, controlling, and directing capacity and sources of income, given the constraints of supply and demand."[2]

APPLYING REVENUE MANAGEMENT

Tranter, Stuart-Hill, and Parker[3] discuss eight steps to applying revenue management.

1. Customer knowledge
2. Market segmentation and selection
3. Internal assessment
4. Competitive analysis
5. Demand forecasting
6. Channel analysis and selection
7. Value-based pricing
8. Channel and inventory management

Many of these steps we have already discussed in this book. In Chapter 5, we looked at customer knowledge as we explored what factors impact their decisions to buy a product. In Chapter 7, we found out how to segment a market and then select the appropriate groups for our product. Internal assessment and the competitive analysis can be found in Chapter 3, as environmental scanning became a part of the Strengths, Weaknesses, Opportunities, and Threats (SWOT) analysis to help us in understanding the relationship between the macro- and the micromarketing environments. Finally, in Chapter 2, we looked at strategic planning to devise systematic processes to decide where we are going and how to get there. **Demand forecasting** is combining our consumer and organizational buying behaviors to decide what our guests will demand so that we can predict our future objectives more clearly.

In the channel analysis and selection, we are analyzing the distribution cost and revenue per channel. This allows companies to decide which channels should have the largest percentage of inventory to achieve the optimal mix of customers. **Channels** are the distribution outlets through which the sellers offer their products and services to their customers, like the travel agents, wholesale tour operators, Internet service providers (ISP), global distribution systems (GDS), or central reservations systems (CRS). Travel agents used to play a very important role in making reservations before the Internet. They served as information sources, practical experience guides, and experts on best prices and availability. However, the Internet took over many of their functions. Now travel agents specialize in specific areas of travel like trips to Japan or adventure travel or cruises or casino trips. An area that is not so well known is the wholesale tour operators. Although *wholesale* refers to the agents who primarily buy and sell in bulk to other wholesalers or retailers, some of these agents now have Web sites for individual travelers. Some specialize in buying inventory that is past the prime selling period. For example, a group tour to Macao casinos from America may still have 20 openings a month before the tour is scheduled to depart. The wholesaler offers to buy 10 of those openings at break-even prices. At this point, the organizers are more concerned about getting any money for the trips since they have

FIGURE 8.3   Anywhere you go today, you can always find a media center to make travel plans.

already paid for the hotels, the airfare, and other miscellaneous items. These wholesalers then offer these packages at around 50%–70% off the original price. If people can travel at a moment's notice, there are truly great packages available for cheap prices.

Many people like to use the Internet Service Providers (ISPs) to see what their alternatives are, to investigate the facilities, to check other people's opinions in special Web sites, and to book reservations. On the other hand, the Global Distribution Systems or GDS are electronic warehouses primarily for organizational buyers like travel agents. The four major GDS are Sabre, Amadeus, Galileo, and Worldspan. Finally, central reservations systems (CRS) are corporate specific because they are set up to take reservations only for all of the properties in their organization. So, for example, you can call a toll-free number and talk to reservations for the Oahu Hilton about March 2 through March 6. They can tell you the availability of rooms, pricing levels, and then book the reservation.

Value-based pricing is the step that researches what is important to potential guests and their perception of what a product is worth. People have an internal value system that determines how much they want to spend. Within this range, they know the maximum they want to spend for a particular product. On the other hand, they also have a feeling for a minimum price. It is generally believed that people will buy anything that is cheap, but that is not necessarily the case. At a certain level, people begin to question the value of the product. For example, if I told you that you could buy a Ferrari for $100, would you take it? Why not? Probably you don't believe that the Ferrari is all there. My students have told me that the Ferrari must be a model car or that the engine is missing with the rest of the body a total mess. Value-based pricing is then the ability of management to offer the product at the optimal price/value relationship.

The final step in the revenue management system is channel and inventory management. *Inventory* is the products or services that are available for sale through various channels. Property management can decide which of these channels it wants to work with in terms of pricing, unit availability, and purchasing rules and restrictions. The most common purchasing rules and restrictions are blocks of time during which rooms cannot be booked. These are usually during high season when the properties are expecting to be full. If they allow bookings during high season, there might be a minimum or maximum length of stay. For example, during Mardi Gras weekend in New Orleans, many hotels require a minimum stay of three days.

IMPORTANCE OF REVENUE MANAGEMENT SYSTEMS

Historically, in order to attract guests, casinos offered comp rooms, F&B, and so forth. It was a human decision based on gut instinct on whether the guest would gamble enough money for the casino to make money. "I remember the good old days when we must have changed rates 20 times a day, but now you don't have to,"[4] said Lyra Beck, corporate director of Hotel Yield and Teleservices at Boyd Gaming. As a result, decisions on comps tended to be made under overgenerous conditions and the hotel rooms and restaurants became just convenient places to stay and eat, but not great revenue generators. As we have discussed, the hotels and restaurants have since grown to become attractions in their own right. They now represent another revenue source to the overall resort. As such, hotels and restaurants have become profit centers, but still the comps are part of their cost of doing business. Therefore, it is important to assess the entire customer profile in order to make a decision about levels of gifts. This is where casino revenue management systems (RMS) differ from regular hospitality operations. Casino **RMS** consider a guest's theoretical future gaming value as well as potential room rate and other possible additional revenue, such as spa use and dining. More often than not, high-rated frequent players are offered a complimentary room or lower room rate, while retail customers (nongamers) are charged amounts that have been calculated to ensure that their value is equal to the gamers' value.

At a casino hotel, gaming changes the stakes in ways that do not apply to nongaming hotels. For example, based on low demand for a night, a nongaming hotel might adjust nightly rates from $110 to $90 in order to capture a little more business. On the other hand, a gaming property might have to decide whether to comp or lose money on the room to obtain a projected $1,000 a night from a gambler. Obviously, the stakes are higher at a casino hotel. Therefore, in a large casino with thousands of rooms, balancing guest profiles, historically predictive patterns, and occupancy rates can translate into countless data and decision points. Although the final decisions about room rates are usually left up to human decision, the sheer volume of data required to make casino revenue management work must be performed by sophisticated software.

> "In the gaming industry there are more revenue streams. Revenue management is a harder thing for a human to do—pretty impossible," said Tim Coleman, V.P. of revenue management for MGM Grand Resorts. "The need for automation is pretty well established. Basic philosophy is to have guest histories compiled and resident in the central reservation systems and then use this data as a forecast for what happens in the future. Revenue management systems import a guest's gaming patterns and resulting value from the casino side, and then factor in forecasted property demand and other variable influences to set room rate and comp availability."[5]

Although the way in which revenue management systems acquire the data they need to make recommendations varies from property to property, there are some basic similarities. At Boyd Gaming, specific amounts wagered by each guest are tracked on the individual casino's management systems. Night audits are followed by the download of this data into the system. At that point, mathematical calculations are used to process this information into data sets and formats that can be read through a user interface. These presentations are then accessible to hotel personnel who wish to know the recommendations for nightly room rates for individual guests and groups.

Unlike regular hotels, because players want to be tracked for their comp status, they come to the casino so "the players segment themselves," said Steven Pinchuk, corporate VP of Revenue Management at Harrah's. "Unlike other applications where we have to segment the market and find reasons for us to do so. These people are worth so much to us, they want to be tracked . . . Since Harrah's implemented revenue management earlier this year, their total revenue has increased more than 50%."[6] However, keep in mind that the best casino revenue management system is only as intelligent as the data entered into it. This means when the RMS produces its specific nightly rate recommendations for guests, managers should have the choice on whether to accept or override them.

> "We try to train our managers in best-practices revenue management," said Tim Coleman, V.P. of revenue management for MGM Grand Resorts. "To make the best decision, our operating people meet daily and set our rate strategies. If sales managers think a group has other values than the system is accounting for, they might go, 'this group should be a higher profile customer for us.' "[7]

HOW DO REVENUE MANAGEMENT SYSTEMS APPLY IN CASINOS?

Las Vegas has been at the forefront of designing its casinos to meet the needs and desires of its targeted guests. Originally, Vegas was the king of cheap meals, breakfasts for $1.99, lunch for $2.99, and a prime rib dinner for $4.99. Rooms were readily comped or provided very cheaply. The intent was to attract men. It was assumed that men were not as concerned about their surroundings and if they could get a cheap meal, so much the better. Gamblers spent their time smoking, drinking, and playing cards at the tables for their whole stay. If they wanted entertainment, there were the nude showgirls at all the nightspots.

However, as Las Vegas grew, it was important to attract more than just the men. Women and families generated more money through longer stays and more volume. As the targeted demographic groups shifted, so did the need for different levels of service, new decors, and higher prices. For example, originally the MGM Grand was green, and had *The Wizard of OZ* as its theme. Giant statues of Dorothy, the Tin Man, and the Cowardly Lion dominated the entryway. Yellow brick roads led tourists to different locations and attractions. To walk into the casino, you entered into a large lion's mouth. This was very impressive for families. Unfortunately, the Asian market was not so impressed. Walking into a lion's mouth was a sign of bad luck. Therefore, they stopped coming to the casino. This was a particular problem since there are many Asian high rollers. The theme had to be changed.

As a result of the shifting demographics, Wynn Las Vegas went after the high end of the market. Their rooms are luxurious, the restaurants have top-of-the-line food quality, the stores in the mall are name brands such as Gucci, Cartier, and Prada, and the prices are high. "What transformed the casino hotel industry's view of room-related revenue was Steve Wynn. Wynn had a vision of the hotel as a centerpiece offering world-class spa, five-star restaurants, and spectacular entertainment," said Lyra Beck, corporate director of Hotel

FIGURE 8.4 Using a good revenue management program to assess new target markets makes good sense and profits.

Source: Images.com.

Yield and Teleservices for Boyd Gaming. Therefore, the hotel is still an amenity in that it is not the reason guests are on property, but it is a huge amenity that now supports itself.

IDENTIFYING PROFITABLE GUESTS

To identify profitable guests coming to the property, casinos need to know who their loyal customers are and then assign them a casino ID.

> "We track every gaming customer's casino activity," said Beck, Boyd Gaming's corporate director of hotel yield and teleservices. "Boyd knows each gamer's name, play history, frequency and value. Our system downloads player data through a link with the casino central processor, together with cash expenditure data from the PMS to create a property-specific forecast embracing customer value as comprehensively as possible. The system also enables our yield managers to input local market factors as an additional point of reference informing the availability recommendations for all guest segments."[8]

When the Reservation department receives a call, they type in the guest's name, player identification (if any), and dates. Instantly, the system provides the appropriate level of comp and room rates.

> "There are no spreadsheets; the system makes the recommendations and our yield managers review them for appropriateness. We do not see the math involved in our system's rate setting and forecasting process," explained Beck. "But as business people we are well qualified to evaluate the forecasts and recommendations for acceptance or modification. Our system handles the calculations quickly so we can focus on fine-tuning strategy as often as necessary."[9]

To transform casino amenities from loss leaders to profit centers, Boyd Gaming conducts weekly rate-setting meetings where managers implement strategies that put the right guest in the right room at the right price. "At Boyd, we conduct frequent sessions where department heads discuss property demand and set room rates. We use a revenue management system from the Rainmaker Group that factors in each guest's forecasted gaming value while analyzing other influences like demand and citywide events to recommend optimized rates for each guest segment."[10] In addition, Boyd Gaming uses the forecasts to help target their promotions with the demand conditions. The forecasts recommend which target market the casino should attract during a specific period.

Other casinos, like the Venetian, say their RMS is unique because it not only forecasts group business but the system also forecasts the length of stay by the day of the week. This is important for maximizing revenue during shoulder periods. Moreover, they believe that the only way to determine the most profitable mix of business to maximize revenue is to forecast demand for the entire inventory.[11]

Pechanga Resort & Casino selected MICROS OPERA RMS because it maximizes bookings by linking guests, corporate accounts, and travel agents directly into its Property Management System (**PMS**) and its Sales & Catering (**S&C**). Pechanga is also the first to implement the OPERA Gaming two-way interface to the Aristocrat OASIS Players Tracking System, which allows authorized staff to request and award comps, monitor and control comp expenses, and provide secure access to real-time details on guest expenditures, stay histories, and gaming statistics. Collecting, maintaining, and analyzing all guest-related data in a single database was a major factor in their selection.[12]

Trump Entertainment Resorts had a manual yielding process before their RMS, so they say there has been dramatic improvement. Rainmaker Group's Revolution Product Suite was selected because they said it was the only commercially available system that incorporated the customer into the revenue management. Total revenue management looks at the holistic value of the customer including his/her history and the gaming components and not just the room rate the customer pays. More specifically the RMS assists in setting room rates and complimentary room hurdles based on a comprehensive profile of each guest. Those room values are based on each guest's total value. Each guest segment is associated with a minimum acceptable value. The bottom line is that every customer is ranked based on his/her estimated gaming worth. For those customers who tend to be high-value customers the key is to predict the demand because the casino can hold special rooms back for them and the system comes into play there. The more data it has the more accurate it becomes. In terms of demand forecast accuracy, Trump is at the point in which it is within plus or minus 3% of the system's forecast.[13]

Before Katrina, Four Diamond IP Casino Resort Spa, Biloxi, Mississippi targeted sports groups and convention business, but these groups did not bring revenue to the casino floor. Now, they use a revenue management software system from the Rainmaker Group to optimize the room rate for each group based on their value to all areas of the enterprise, including the casino. The system estimates the total property profitability of each guest segment by analyzing player gaming information and other data to set rates. The system's rates are based on historical gaming performance and include forecasts of additional revenue from dining, spa, and other sources. To ensure that they accept the most valuable groups, they run every group through the profitability analysis to forecast

FIGURE 8.5 Using revenue management strategies can help you determine who should have a standard room and who should be upgraded.

its theoretical revenue contribution to the company. In addition, other property departments use the system to forecast appropriate staffing levels.[14]

Observers of the gaming industry believe that Harrah's is so successful because the company has an intimate understanding of its customers. Harrah's hotels, for example had a remarkable 95% occupancy rate in 2003. More remarkably, the company turns down twice as many requests for reservations as it accepts, which is why it continues to invest in new hotel rooms. "It's not about filling each room," explains David Norton, senior vice president of Relationship Marketing at Harrah's. "It's about maxing out the profit from each room." Harrah's launched a hotel revenue management system in 2001, enabling it to optimize the profitability of its hotel rooms through a combination of gaming revenue and room rate. RMS forecasts occupancy at a detailed customer-segment level based on historical and projected trends, and makes a decision in real time about whether a customer should get into the hotel and at what room rate, based on the customer's profile in the data warehouse, which is based on National Cash Register (NCR) Teradata technology. The customer will get a consistent answer whether booking over the phone or online at Harrahs.com. Patrons who play a lot get sweetheart deals. They also tend to get lots of mail. "About 75% of our revenue comes from direct-marketing offers," "If we didn't do it, our revenues would tank."[15]

HOW SUCCESSFUL ARE THE REVENUE MANAGEMENT SYSTEMS?

"Since Boyd installed its current system in early 2006, they have reduced stay–no play and other low-profit customers by 23%. Additionally, comp expenses have been reduced 35% and have increased cash revenue 4%,"[16] according to Lyra Beck, corporate director of

Hotel Yield and Teleservices at Boyd Gaming. Rayneet Bhandari, senior VP of Revenue Strategy and Systems said, "In the 6 months the system has been in place at Trump's hotels, the company has generated close to $4.5 million in total cash revenue, which is the equivalent of a 6.5% year over year increase in the total revenue basis."[17] "With the help of a new revenue management system, our **ADR** (Average Daily Rate) is up 300%,"[18] said Robert Brigham, VP of Hotel Operations, Four Diamond IP Casino Resort Spa, Biloxi, Mississippi.

CULTURAL SHIFT IN THINKING

One of the major changes with revenue management is that it is a way of doing business. It requires a cultural shift in thinking.[19] Therefore, T. Farley offers three suggestions to help shift focus.

1. Shift your focus from occupancy and rate to profitability. Instead of thinking of each unit (such as hotel, F&B, spa, etc.) as stand-alone items, think about it in terms of profitability. Gary Loveman, chairman, CEO, and president of Harrah's Entertainment, Inc., told Wall Street analysts their metrics do not fit the casino gaming industry. He said, "Look at gaming profit per room and gaming win per room instead of ADR (Average Daily Rate) and occupancy."[20]
2. Move from silos to integrated departments. **Silos** refer to individual units that stand alone. Let RM teams report through sales and marketing instead of operations. This creates clear communication between the casino Sales and Marketing department, revenue managers, and hotel operators.
3. Recognize that a day in the life of a revenue manager has changed from crunching numbers to strategic thinking.

Conclusion

Revenue management is the new wave of pricing strategy. For casinos, it combines all the different aspects of the resort into one calculated database. It allows all the different revenue streams to have a part in a gambler's spending package, and therefore his/her worth to the company. In addition, it takes casino comps from the days when a pit boss studied a gambler and figured out in his head how much the person was worth to the new quantifiable complex algorithms that now represent a gambler. To some who remember the good old days when you finessed management in order to get comped, now casinos are impersonal and too complex. To others who grew up in the computer age of technology, it is just another way to gather together all the data that is out there to make the most effective, profitable decisions.

Key Words

Review Questions

1. Explain the early pricing strategies of casinos.
2. Discuss some of the contemporary pricing strategies of casinos.
3. Discuss the many aspects of defining revenue management.
4. List and discuss the eight ways of applying revenue management.
5. Detail the importance of revenue management systems.
6. Explain how revenue management systems apply to casino operations.
7. Detail some of the ways of identifying profitable guests.
8. Discuss the levels of success of various revenue management systems.
9. Discuss the cultural shift in thinking.

Endnotes

1. Tranter, K. A., Stuart-Hill, T., and Parker, J. (2009). *Introduction to Revenue Management for the Hospitality Industry.* Upper Saddle River, NJ: Prentice Hall Publishers, 24.
2. Ibid, 9.
3. Ibid.
4. Shaw, R. (2007). Hotel gaming raises revenue management stakes. *Hotel & Motel Management.* Retrieved May 13, 2008, from http://www.hotelmotel.com/hotelmotel/content/.
5. Ibid.
6. Ibid.
7. Ibid.
8. Boyd Gaming hits "jackpot" with revenue management strategy (2006). Retrieved May 13, 2008, from http://www.hotel-online.com/News/PR2006/Sep05_TheRainmakerGroup.html.
9. Ibid.
10. Beck, L. (2006). Revenue a different game for casino properties. Retrieved May 13, 2008, from http://www.lhonline.com/mag/revenue_different_game.
11. The Venetian Resort Hotel Casino selects IDeaS Revenue Management. Las Vegas Resort Casino selects IDeaS after two year search. (2002). Retrieved May 13, 2008, from http://www.hotel-online.com/News/PR2002_2nd/June02_VenetianIDeaS.html.
12. Press release (2007). Pechanga Resort & Casino selects the MICROS OPERA Enterprise Solution. Columbia, MD: MICROS Systems, Inc.
13. Shaw, R. (2007). Hotel gaming raises revenue management stakes. *Hotel & Motel Management.* Retrieved May 13, 2008, from http://www.hotelmotel.com/hotelmotel/content/.
14. IP Casino Resort success story (2007, August 22). *Casino City Times.* Retrieved May 13, 2008, from http://www.casinocitytimes.com/news/article.cfm?contentID=168130.
15. Goff, J. (2004). Businesses are deploying analytical software to get a better fix on customer behavior. Retrieved May 13, 2008, from http://www.cfo.com/printable/article.cfm/3014815/c_2983272?f=options.
16. Shaw, R. (2007). Hotel gaming raises revenue management stakes. *Hotel & Motel Management.* Retrieved May 13, 2008, from http://www.hotelmotel.com/hotelmotel/content/.
17. Ibid.
18. IP Casino Resort success story (2007, August 22). *Casino City Times.* Retrieved May 13, 2008, from http://www.casinocitytimes.com/news/article.cfm?contentID=168130.
19. Farley, T. (2008). Follow the money: 10 years of profit optimization progress pays off for operators. Retrieved May 13, 2008, from http://www.hoteljobresource.com/news.
20. Ibid.

CHAPTER 9

PLACE—THE IMPORTANCE OF CHANNELS, LOCATION, AND TRANSPORTATION

KATHRYN HASHIMOTO

Learning Objectives

1. To provide an understanding of how channels of distribution affect the operation of casinos[1]
2. To explore the effect of accessibility on the operations of casinos
3. To detail how a casino's physical location affects its operations
4. To detail how the distance between casinos affects their operations
5. To detail how a casino fits into its market affects its operations
6. To learn the importance of different modes of transportation to a casino's operations
7. To understand the history of waterways, ground, and air transportation to a casino's operation
8. To learn about the importance of location and transportation in casinos
9. To understand the importance of the originating state of visitors to casinos
10. To understand the importance of the participation region of visitors to casinos
11. To learn about the impacts of transportation on casino operations

Chapter Outline

INTRODUCTION

So far, we have been discussing things that a casino can control, such as product and pricing strategies. Now, we will explore some of the implications of a casino's location and the different transportation options to get guests to and from the site. Gaming, as we have seen in many chapters, is a proven tourist attraction. As a result, gaming has become widespread in the United States, and most of the states have legalized casino gaming in one form or another regardless of the casino's location. What has taken place in Las Vegas and Atlantic City over the past few decades has been repeated on a smaller scale in new gaming jurisdictions throughout the country.

In the United States, casinos have been introduced to Native American reservations and small mining towns to enhance local economies, and this development of casinos has spread throughout the states after Native American reservations in Connecticut and South Dakota proved their potential economic value. Because people like to gamble, casinos and surrounding attractions bring visitors to a region. Casinos not only draw new visitors to a place, but they also prompt visitors in surrounding areas to stay longer. However, depending on the channels working with the casino, accessibility of the location, and the modes of transportation available to get to the site, a casino can be more, or less, profitable.

CHANNELS OF DISTRIBUTION

One of the factors of place is called **channels of distribution**. This refers to the number of intermediaries that the product goes through from casino to guest. As the number of distribution channels increases, so does the price, because of the markup (the percentage of the price used for profit). In industries that produce tangible goods, distribution channels move the product from the factory to the customers. However, in the gaming industry, the distribution channels move the customer to the casino, since the location is fixed. The channels can be either internal or external. Internal channels are employees, such as casino hosts, and branch offices that are controlled by the casino. These people create various packages to invite the guests to the casino. If you are a high roller, then a host might offer you a junket, which is an all-expense-paid trip to the casino for special events such as a big boxing match or a golf tournament.

External channels are businesses such as tour operators and junket operators. Travel agents and wholesalers make it easier for the casino to reach some guests because they are closer to the client, so it is beneficial to use them. For example, a person who lives in Hong Kong may want to come to Las Vegas to gamble. Perhaps this person has never been to the United States and so he/she is reluctant to trust the trip to his/her knowledge and experience. A trusted travel agent who has been to Las Vegas might be a welcome source of information. The agent can recommend places to see, casinos to visit, and restaurants and shows at which to make reservations. In addition, the tour operator may be able to offer a group tour so that the language barrier will not be an issue; there will always be someone who speaks the same language who can guide him/her. In this way, the visit can be more enjoyable because all the details are handled before anyone leaves home.

However, today it is more likely that a person can simply turn on his/her computer and scan all the current information on tours, flights, hotels, and attractions. He/she can look at restaurant reviews online and book a dinner reservation in an instant. By looking at several Web sites, hotel rates can be determined for specific travel dates and then compared to the casino resorts already selected. It is easy if you know how. On the other hand, if someone was born before the age of computers, the old-fashioned way may be the best.

Understanding the different channels of distribution that are available is important so that casino managers can decide how to handle them. If you think that the channel member is very good for business, then you might want to offer them special prices so that they will be able to sell a lot of packages and it will be a lucrative deal for them and for the casino. When assessing channel members, there are three key factors: cost, control, and communications. The channels must be cost effective. Some casinos have gone out of business because the compensation they paid the channel members was too high above their theoretical win. It is important to remain in control. Junket operators especially tend to have a loyal following of gamblers, which causes friction when the casino wants to shift that loyalty to themselves. Sometimes high rollers become attached to their casino host. As a result, if a casino host moves to another location, the high roller may follow. Therefore, it is important that management should be involved in greeting and entertaining players to build up player loyalty for the house. The third key to effective channel management is communication. Casinos may set up a package and promote it to travel agents. When the package changes, the changes have to be communicated effectively to hundreds of travel agents. Some agents will lose or misfile the message and as a result, sell the old package, which sometimes results in the casino not meeting the guest's expectations. Constant reinforcement and reminders will help. In addition, it is always important to check the trip conditions to make sure both you and the travel agents are selling the same package and pricing.

Because few Native American casinos and charitable bingo halls are large enough to include substantial marketing programs, most marketing to bingo players originate at the equipment level. Some suppliers, such as Arrow, provide operators with customer-service tips and marketing ideas on their Web sites or through seminars at trade shows. Others, such as Multimedia Games, conduct their own player promotions over broadband networks linking their progressive games.[2] As a result, channel members can be very helpful, especially if your casino is in a remote location.

ACCESSIBILITY

"Build it, and they will come" has been the predominant thought as America embraced gambling fever. This might have been true prior to the late 1970s when casino facilities were limited in number and primarily found in the Las Vegas and Atlantic City areas. Because there was one in the West and one in the East, there were no major competitive problems. People traveled to casinos even if accessibility was not convenient because no other places were available. This has changed as more casinos are opened in many other states and they are within short distances to nearby communities. In addition, communities, along with casinos work to build the infrastructure necessary to provide convenient accessibility to potential visitors. Place is concerned with all the decisions involved in getting the right product to the target markets or in the case of casinos, getting the right market to the product.

> One of the strongest marketing aspects of a locals' casino is convenience and we have it. I know because I hear it a thousand times a day. The Palms is easy to get into and easy to get out of. All the amenities that locals want such as movie theaters, buffet, coffee shop, race and sports book, spa, and wide variety of games are here. In fact, locals patronize it more than I originally planned. The Palms has become a high-end locals place and once they get here, they find there is no reason to leave.
>
> —George Maloof, president and owner, Palms Casino Resort[3]

Casino Locations

There are casinos located in or near metropolitan areas such as Las Vegas, Tunica, Mississippi, and Atlantic City, which are desirable places to spend your vacation. There are many tourist attractions in these areas. So, the location automatically draws tourists and

FIGURE 9.1   Parking lots need to be easy to get into and easy to leave.

locals. For example, people might go to Las Vegas and also go to the Hoover Dam or the Grand Canyon, which are major attractions in their own right. In addition, it is easy to get to these cities because they are located near major hubs for the airlines so it is quite likely that you can get a direct flight. Also, the airport is located nearby so mass transit or taxi service is available. Major highways have been constructed over the years that make drive-in traffic easy, so the casinos are accessible. In 2007, there were seven casinos generating revenues over $1 billion (with St. Louis just under). Of course, Las Vegas was first with over $6.7 billion, followed by Atlantic City at $4.9 billion. However, Chicagoland, Connecticut, Detroit, and Tunica and Biloxi, Mississippi, were running between 1 and 2.6 billion in revenue.[4] As you can see, all of these casinos have locations near metropolitan areas.

On the other hand, casinos in rural (or suburban) areas such as Silver City, Deadwood, South Dakota; Black Hawk, Colorado; and many Native American reservations are not noted as destination attractions. As an example, Deadwood is located in the heart of the Black Hills. In order to fly in to the nearest airport, a person must make several connections. Then, Deadwood is about 400 miles away from a large hub airport. Even if there is a regional airport 50 miles away from Deadwood, the majority of the people still drive because the regional airport is inconvenient. Casinos on most Native American reservations are also more inconvenient for air travelers because of their isolated locations and limited transportation infrastructure. For instance, Prairie Winds Casino on the Pine Ridge Sioux Indian Reservation in South Dakota has only one main highway in. As a result, they are between the fifteenth and twentieth position of revenue spending in casinos. Additional casinos that are in rural areas and are in the higher end of the top 20 revenue generators are places like Lake Charles (Louisiana); Laughlin and Black Hawk (Colorado); Council Bluff (Iowa); and Charles Town (West Virginia). Keep in mind these still generate revenues from $463–$640 million. Not a bad living for isolated towns.

Casino locations can be categorized in two ways: according to the distance of travel from home, and target markets. Markets for the casino industry, in terms of location, can

FIGURE 9.2 Deadwood, South Dakota, located in the Black Hills, 400 miles from the nearest airport hub.

Source: Peter Frischmuth/argus/Peter Arnold Inc.

be divided into three categories: the convenience market, the transit market, and the pleasure market. The **convenience market** falls in the local or regional casino category since, as the name says, it is convenient for the visitors to get there. The transit market and the pleasure market fall in the nonlocal casino category.

By Distances

It may not be possible to identify a local and nonlocal customer. However, in general, a tourist is defined as a person who travels at least 100 miles from home. Therefore, nonlocal casinos could be defined as places that are farther than 100 miles from where their target markets live. By default then, local casinos can be defined as casinos that mainly serve people traveling less than 100 miles from home. For example, casinos in Las Vegas can be categorized as nonlocal casinos because a large percentage of guests fly in, while casinos in small towns or on Native American reservations could be categorized as local casinos since these casinos draw the majority of their visitors from the region. However, even in Las Vegas, there are local casinos because they draw gamblers from the surrounding areas. Especially on Frontier Street downtown, there are local casinos.

> We knew going in we didn't want a themed hotel. We wanted guests who would appreciate a smaller, more intimate hotel with no hassle or long lines and who didn't want to walk long corridors to their rooms. Our location has turned out to be perfect because we're just off the Strip where we can attract customers but close enough to the neighborhoods for locals. . . . we're still finding our way and are discovering new customers with special events. But the one thing that's working for us and it's a theory that has been around for years, is location, location, location. Combine that with the convenience of getting here and it becomes a solid marketing tool.[5]—George Maloof, president and owner, Palms Casino Resort.

For visitors from the East Coast of the United States, the bulk of casinos are along the Jersey shore in Atlantic City, and Indian casinos in other inland communities. Even though the Native American casinos are inland and more difficult to access, the northeast corridor has the densest population in the United States. For example, Atlantic City is a one- to four-hour drive (depending on traffic) from Philadelphia (1.5 million), New York City (19.3 million), and Hartford/New Haven (386 thousand).[6] Therefore, even if you can attract only 1% of the people each year, that still leaves a lot of people to attract and they can easily drive the distance. In addition, there are many hubs for people to fly in to get to Atlantic City.

The Mississippi and Missouri rivers are home to an increasing number of riverboat casinos, and Midwesterners are becoming regular visitors to these riverboat casinos. Small town casinos in South Dakota and Colorado became popular destinations for visitors to the Rockies in Colorado and the Black Hills, in South Dakota. Native American casinos as new travel destinations in many states attract local or regional residents and provide gambling for residents who would otherwise travel long distances.

By Markets

The convenience markets are located within easy driving distance from major urban areas but are not convenient by airplane. Many Native American casinos in California and Minnesota are examples of the convenience markets. **The pleasure markets** may require long-distance travel and need more than gambling facilities. Casinos in the pleasure market provide more lodging facilities, various restaurants, and additional recreational amenities. Atlantic City, New Jersey; Tunica and Biloxi, Mississippi; Foxwoods, Connecticut; or Las Vegas, Nevada fall in this category. **The transit markets** are located between the pleasure markets and the convenience markets. These markets have neither additional facilities nor easy access for air travelers. These markets do not tend to focus on one specific potential market; instead, they focus on markets that have multiple characteristics. Visitors to these markets are not gambling oriented but they are there for other activities; the casino is a supplementary activity for them. Casinos in South Dakota, Colorado, Iowa, North Dakota, or casinos on Native American reservations fall in this category.

Since gaming has become acceptable as a leisure or recreational activity in American society, more people tend to travel to casinos. It is clear that there are more auto travelers in the convenience markets compared to other markets. There are fewer air travelers in the transit markets compared to other markets because of the lack of air transportation infrastructure for the transit markets. Another reason can be that travelers in the transit markets tend to visit multiple places during their trips. Travelers in the pleasure markets need to spend more money for the trips than travelers in other markets because of long-distance travel, lodging, and food and beverage. Characteristics in each category are described in Table 9.1.

TABLE 9.1   Characteristics of Markets.[7]

Transit Market	Convenience Market	Pleasure Market
• Travelers tend to have other major destinations	• Travel destinations	• Travel destinations
• Small or medium size casinos because of a lack of mass travelers	• Small, medium, or large size casinos because of mass travelers	• Large casinos
• Tend to be sensitive to seasons—more traffic during the peak season	• Tend to not be sensitive to seasons	• Tend to be somewhat sensitive to the seasons
• Tend to have natural attractions such as national or state parks or other cultural attractions	• Tend to have more activities/amenities	• Tend to have more amenities and activities besides gaming • Tend to have natural and man-made attractions
• Tend to have limited lodging facilities	• Tend to have limited lodging facilities	• Tend to have various lodging facilities for various markets • Tend to have more luxurious lodging facilities
• Tend to be located in rural areas	• Tend to be located in urban or suburban areas close to metropolitan areas	• Tend to be located in urban or suburban areas
• Tend to have accessibility limited to ground transportation	• Tend to have easy accessibility by ground transportation but not air transportation	• Tend to have easy accessibility by both ground and air transportation

TRANSPORTATION AND CASINOS

People traveled by horses or by foot in earlier years. Railroads and waterways became popular for long-distance travelers until the automobile was introduced. This shifted the location of hotels from along the rivers or stagecoach routes to towns that had train stations or towns that had a great potential to bring railroads. Communities on the routes became popular with new infrastructure and communities with lodging facilities were able to attract more travelers and settlers to the communities. Hotels were built close to train stations, stagecoach depots, or waterway landings. As there were an increasing number of people coming to the communities, these communities began to seek more entertainment activities along with hotel development. As lodging facilities were built and used for travelers and residents, hotels became places for gathering. As hotels became a social place, other amenities such as casinos and bars were needed in order to attract travelers. Gambling was offered in these hotels or bars.

Today, people travel using different modes of transportation: automobile, bus, train, or airplane. As the tourism industry develops and people tend to have more disposable income and time, additional demands will be made on transportation. In general, the choice of transportation is a combination of length of trip, number of people in the group, disposable time, and disposable income for travel. In order to meet the demands of travelers, regardless of location, consideration for accessibility is a key factor. There is no doubt that gaming generates travel; however, casinos must identify ways to attract potential travelers who have limited time in order to be better positioned in the very competitive tourism communities.

A multifaceted transportation infrastructure provides easy access to casino facilities. Casino products have been spread out to all segments of the market. It has been estimated that there is a casino within 300 miles of any urban area in the United States and 150 miles from Atlantic City, New Jersey. With casinos, as well as other forms of tourism development,

FIGURE 9.3

Source: Eugene Gordon/Pearson Education/PH College.

transportation is an important concern, especially in rural small towns that have been converted from mining towns to gaming establishments or small towns on Indian reservations throughout the country. Communities that provide casinos as a major travel product also provide convenient multiple-transportation modes, while communities that provide casinos as a supplementary travel product provide limited transportation. The result is more nonlocal casino users in communities with casino-oriented areas and more local casino users in communities with casino-supported areas.

MODES OF TRANSPORTATION

As people travel to experience new environments with some excitement, and the tourism industry increases along with increasing disposable income and time, the mode of transportation has been shifted from cheaper to faster and more convenient. Looking at the various modes of passenger transportation, people traveled by various modes of transportation from on foot to riding in a supersonic aircraft. As the tourism industry becomes globalized, people look for travel destinations that meet their expectations from natural sites to cities that provide multiple attractions. Air travel dominates long-distance and middle-distance tourism while the automobile dominates short-distance tourism. It is important to understand that the foundation of tourism is people, transportation, and destination. Destinations that provide multiple-transportation modes have an advantage of attracting more visitors compared to areas that provide limited transportation modes.

There are a variety of ways by which people can travel between multiple destinations. People consider availability, frequency, cost, speed, and comfort in the process of selecting a travel mode. It is indicated that destinations that provide various transportation modes that move passengers quickly from one place to another comfortably, frequently, and at a low price are better positioned in the marketplace. Today, there are three major modes of passenger transportation that people can choose to travel by: air, ground, and water. The majority of travelers still use ground transportation, even though the number of air travelers has rapidly increased. Multiple-transportation options have great affect on people's destination choices, along with many other factors. These factors include affordability, time, and whether or not the mode of transport is well marketed and convenient.

Waterways

Americans extended the frontiers of the nation in a relatively short period of time, from the shores of the Great Lakes in the north, to the Mississippi in the west, and to the Gulf of Mexico in the south. Transportation was supplemented by extensive use of the many miles of natural waterways, extending inland from the coast and spreading throughout the interior of the country. Transportation developed along the waterways that provided easy and fast access to casinos as water transportation developed. As early as the first decade of the nineteenth century, traffic with New Orleans had developed in the towns and settlements on the Ohio and Mississippi rivers. The introduction of the steamboat on inland rivers in the early 1800s marked the beginning of important traffic by packet boats.

As transportation developed along the waterways in the earlier years, gaming activities became a part of the amenities on passenger riverboats along the Mississippi and the Ohio. Before the first steamship was designed, and around the same time the steam engine was first used in trains, water transportation modes had been used for exploration,

FIGURE 9.4

commerce, people transportation, and some leisure travel. The modes of water transportation consisted of ocean liners crossing the oceans and riverboats cruising rivers. Today, the ship remains an important passenger transportation mode in its role as only a ferry service. Waterway transportation has become less popular compared to **ground transportation** such as railroad and automobiles. Just as the automobile led to the demise of the train, the introduction of commercial air services made the use of ships as a mode of passenger transportation fade away. Instead, cruising has taken the place of scheduled liner services and gambling has come on board again.

Ground

Rail transportation was the major mode of travel in the United States until 1920. As the Hosmer Report in 1958 indicated, its role has been lessened from when it was introduced in the United States. Rail travel became more limited because its infrastructure had not advanced, as had highway infrastructure. Current development of high-speed trains will improve the railway's role in regions that are connected to highly populated areas. Trains have been perceived as slow in reaching destinations, relatively inflexible with regard to departure and arrival times, and costly. When the automobile began to make inroads in the 1920s and 1930s, the railways began to lose their market share to the automobile. Roadside accommodations and services became far more important than accommodations for train riders to the city centers. Since the United States Interstate Highway System started in 1954, about 90% of the U.S. cities with populations larger than 50,000 are serviced by Interstate highways. As a result, the convenience of the automobile has minimized other modes of transportation, including the train.

The automobile provided accessibility for travelers to many areas that travelers could not reach by other transportation modes. It allowed people to travel from the Atlantic to the Pacific over land. People started to travel more and to longer distances, stopping at several places on their journey. Casino developments were heavily influenced by the development of auto transportation in the United States. As an example, Las Vegas started as a small desert railroad town. The first settlement in Las Vegas can be traced back to 1829. This small town became the casino capital of the world since it legalized gambling in 1931. Casino gambling grew rapidly after World War II, along with the development of transportation and accommodation facilities. The automobile is still the dominating mode of passenger transportation even after the introduction of air transportation. Shifting the development of transportation from waterways to railroads, and then to highways and airways changed the development of casinos from water based to land based.

Air

The first manned air flight, by the Wright brothers in Kitty Hawk, North Carolina in 1903, was in a machine that flew only about 40 yards. After that, air transportation was developed mainly for military, freight, and mail purposes. It is important to understand that the early planes were no faster than trains over the same routes, and were much less reliable. Since there was no incentive for the airlines to carry passengers, the U.S. airlines counted on the government's mail contracts to survive. The modern airline industry was established in 1930 with four major airlines, United, American, Eastern, and Trans World Airlines (TWA). Air transportation has taken on an important transportation role as international and intercontinental travelers increased.

Since the U.S. airline industry was deregulated in 1978, scheduled airlines were forced to reduce prices to attract the traveler; however, this caused a lack of air transportation services for small communities. Air transportation is particularly important for the current casino gaming industry as the market has expanded to include business travelers. Many casinos, especially those in Las Vegas, are equipped with meeting facilities in order to attract the increasing number of convention attendees. In the airline industry, the more people fly, the more flights can be offered, and the lower prices can be because of lower per passenger operating costs. The more competition there is among the airlines, the lower the price will be for their customers. When there are hub airports, it is easier for travelers to make long-distance trips to casinos far away.

IMPORTANCE OF LOCATION AND TRANSPORTATION

The success or failure of a casino is often a function of the old real estate adage of "location, location, location." This advice holds equally true for Native American casinos. Witness the proliferation of tribal gaming operations since passage of the Federal Indian Gaming Regulatory Act in 1988. Since then, only two casinos, Foxwoods and Mohegan Sun, have achieved the stunning success so often sought after by tribal owners. The popularity of these two Connecticut gaming properties owes much to their being situated in the heavily trafficked Northeast, near the population centers of New York City, Boston, and Providence. But the majority of Native American casinos around the country haven't been so blessed with their locations. In Wisconsin, where 11 tribes operate 17 casinos, almost all are on reservations in the sparsely populated northern half of the state. Consequently, in the early 1990s, some Wisconsin tribes began to look south to open casinos closer to more lucrative markets near Milwaukee and northern Illinois. These tribes were hoping to make use of a provision in Indian Gaming Regulatory Act (IGRA) that lets the U.S. Interior

Department take what has historically been nontribal land into trust as an initial step in the development of a casino. Despite this legal possibility, only two on-reservation casinos have stayed open in the United States since 1989, with dozens of applications to open others ensnared in the tangle of local and state politics.

The casinos that are located in metropolitan areas are more likely to provide sufficient **transportation infrastructure** such as interstate highways, major airports, scheduled air services, and so forth. Examples of these casinos in urban areas include Atlantic City and Las Vegas. Casinos in the areas that have a multifaceted transportation infrastructure have stronger marketing advantages compared to the ones in rural areas such as mining towns or Indian reservations in the Midwest. Long-distance travelers tend to not make trips to rural casinos unless those casinos are located on the way to their destinations, or have popular attractions in surrounding areas. This indicates that each casino location targets markets for either short-distance travelers who might be described as local or regional, long-distance travelers, or transit travelers who visit casinos on the way to their final destinations.

People go to every corner of the world to fulfill their desires. They drive hours and hours or they fly long distances to casinos not only for gambling but also for other activities or attractions. Casinos were accepted mainly as an activity for adults only but recently have begun to attract all age groups, and these destinations provide what people want to experience regardless of their age and income. Since casino gambling was legalized in Las Vegas, Nevada, it has brought in millions of visitors from every corner of the world. Las Vegas is a fully developed tourist destination, served by 60 major airlines and McCarran International Airport, which averages over 800 flights daily, and brings in millions of visitors, including 4 million international visitors. Laughlin, Nevada, developed from a town that had 95 people when it introduced casino gambling in late 1960. While visitors from all over the world visit Las Vegas, Laughlin attracts nearby prosperous visitors coming from surrounding states. Compared to Las Vegas, the majority of visitors to Laughlin are vacationers who use ground transportation modes such as recreation vehicles, charter buses, or personal automobiles.

Atlantic City is located on the shore of the Atlantic Ocean, and provides multiple-tourism products along with a well-developed transportation system to provide convenient accessibility for nearby residents. The city is also located a short distance from other highly populated areas such as New York City, and Baltimore. Atlantic City has been a tourism destination since its foundation in the 1850s. It was once a premier resort city on the East Coast of the United States with resort hotels catering to middle- and upper middle-class Americans. With the introduction of the automobile and the improvement of highway infrastructure along with lodging developments in other areas, Atlantic City experienced a decline in visitors until casino gaming was introduced. Atlantic City has since successfully promoted short-duration motor coach tours to increase the number of casino travelers.

By Originating States

A Harrah's study[8] shows that visitors to casinos are usually residents of neighboring areas (states). For example, as Table 9.2 indicates, residents in Alabama visit the Gulf Coast, Indian reservations, and Tunica in Mississippi, and residents in Iowa and Nebraska visit Iowa and South Dakota Indian reservations, and Quad cities, Council Bluff, and Iowa

TABLE 9.2   Casino Destinations by Originated States.[9]

State	Originated States
Alabama	Gulf Cost, MS; Indian reservations; Tunica, MS
Arizona	Arizona Indian; Las Vegas; Laughlin, NV
Arkansas	Shreveport, LA; Bossier City, IA; Tunica, MS
California	Las Vegas; California Indian
Colorado	Colorado; Las Vegas
Connecticut	Atlantic City; Connecticut Indian; Las Vegas
Delaware	Atlantic City; Delaware; Las Vegas
Florida	Cruise ships; Florida Indian; Gulf Coast, MS; Las Vegas
Georgia	Cherokee, NC; Gulf Coast, MS; Las Vegas
Idaho	Idaho Indian; Las Vegas; other Nevada
Illinois	Chicago area; Las Vegas; St. Louis
Indiana	Chicago area; Las Vegas; Southern IL
Iowa	Iowa Indian; river boats; Quad Cities/Council Bluffs, IA
Kansas	Kansas City, MO; Kansas Indian; Las Vegas
Kentucky	Southern IL; Tunica, MS
Louisiana	Gulf coast, MS; Lake Charles, New Orleans, Shreveport/Bossier City, LA
Maine*	N/A
Maryland	Atlantic City; Delaware
Massachusetts	Connecticut Indian; Rhode Island
Michigan	Detroit/Windsor, MI
Minnesota	Las Vegas; Minnesota Indian
Mississippi	Gulf Coast and Tunica, MS; Vicksburg,MS,
Missouri	Kansas City, MO; St. Louis
Montana*	N/A
Nebraska	Quad Cities/Council Bluffs, IA; South Dakota Indian
Nevada	Las Vegas; Reno
New Hampshire	Atlantic City; Connecticut Indian
New Jersey	Atlantic City; Las Vegas
New Mexico	Las Vegas; New Mexico Indian
New York	Atlantic City; Connecticut
North Carolina	Atlantic City; Cherokee, NC
North Dakota	Minnesota Indian; North Dakota Indian
Ohio	Detroit/Windsor, Ontario; Las Vegas; Southern Illinois; West Virginia
Oklahoma	Las Vegas; Oklahoma Indian; Tunica, MS
Oregon	Las Vegas: Oregon Indian
Pennsylvania	Atlantic City: West Virginia
Rhode Island	Connecticut Indian: Rhode Island
South Carolina	Cherokee, NC; Las Vegas
South Dakota	North Dakota Indian; South Dakota Indian
Tennessee	Cherokee, NC; Southern Illinois; Tunica, MS
Texas	Lake Charles, LA; Las Vegas: Shreveport/Bossier City, LA
Utah	Las Vegas
Vermont*	N/A
Virginia	Atlantic City; Las Vegas; West Virginia
Washington	Las Vegas; Washington Indian
West Virginia	Las Vegas; West Virginia
Wisconsin	Las Vegas; Wisconsin Indian
Wyoming	

*Samples are too small.

riverboats. Destinations that provide multiple megacasinos and other activities are still favorite destinations for visitors across the nation. Communities that provide megacasinos such as Las Vegas, Atlantic City, and Native American casinos in Connecticut or Tunica attract visitors from many areas throughout the country, while communities that provide limited casino facilities attract locals or visitors from surrounding regions. Las Vegas is accessible from all communities in the United States while Deadwood or riverboat casinos in Iowa are limited to the surrounding communities.

By Participation Region

Dividing the country into census regions, the West region has the highest gambling participation rate at 32%. The rate in the North central region where commercial or Native American gambling is available in most states is second at 25%, the Northeast at 19%, and the South at 24%.[10] States that had participation rates below the national averages are states that provide fewer casinos compared to states that rate above the national average. For example, States that rated higher than 35% in the year 2003 were Arizona, California, Colorado, Connecticut, Louisiana, Massachusetts, Minnesota, Mississippi, Missouri, Nebraska, New Jersey, Nevada, North Dakota, Rhode Island, and South Dakota. These states either have their own, or are close to multiple-casino facilities, regardless of type and size, that people can easily visit. For example, people from Massachusetts, Connecticut, and Rhode Island may have convenient access to casinos in Connecticut, while people from Maine, New Hampshire, Vermont, and West Virginia do not have convenient access to casinos in Connecticut. As Table 9.2 indicates, many areas of the country are undersupplied by casino gambling opportunities, and many residents are required to travel significant distances, often across state lines, to visit a casino.

The Impacts of Transportation

Location is one of the most important factors in any business. It measures the business' potential market placement and its characteristics. However, in terms of casino development, the impact of locations can be minimized when sufficient transportation infrastructure is provided for travelers. Interstate highways may bring more short-distance travelers and transients to different destinations, while larger airports attract more segment travelers from other regions or countries. People tend to choose the nearest gaming centers that meet their expectations unless they use casinos as their vacation destinations. In the selection of casinos as travel destinations, travel decisions are based on destination type, cost, safety, seasonality, and accessibility.[11] Since accessibility to destination casinos, regardless of location, is vital to the success of casino operations, transportation plays an important role in the gaming industry.

Comparisons between areas that have convenient transportation infrastructure and those areas that do not might be significant. Areas that provide convenient transportation infrastructure such as interstate highways, airports, and scheduled air service may be attractive markets for long vacationers whose destinations are casino facilities. Areas that are located in densely populated areas, which are more likely to provide advanced transportation infrastructure, may attract the day-trippers whose destinations are casino facilities that also provide other activities such as shopping. These areas also focus on mass tourism that brings visitors from multiple markets, while areas that do not provide advanced transportation infrastructure attract alternative tourism that focuses on a single market.

Conclusion

In the United States, gaming is being introduced to Indian reservations and rural communities to create economic development. As new casinos are introduced in many states as Indian casinos, land-based casinos, racetracks, dockside casinos, or riverboat casinos, the impact of gaming on tourism and the local economy becomes evident. Given the current growth in gaming, it is safe to predict that it will continue to play a role in tourism and economic development. Rural areas around the world are facing everything from depopulation to changes in government policy on agriculture and a lack of economic resources.

In many of these places, tourism has been seen as a solution, a way of rejuvenating rural economies and providing a new future for rural communities. The development of casinos has become a solution regardless of surrounding areas. This development of casinos will continue to grow, in not only the United States but also other countries. Casinos located in the areas with well-developed transportation infrastructure attract destination visitors from long distances who fly or drive because of a casino's convenient accessibility, in addition to visitors from the region.

Key Words

Channels of distribution *111*
External channels *112*
The convenience market *115*

The pleasure market *115*
The transit market *116*
Ground transportation *119*

Transportation infrastructure *121*

Review Questions

1. Explain how channels of distribution affect the operation of casinos.
2. Detail the effects of accessibility on the operations of casinos.
3. Explain how a casino's physical location affects its operations.
4. Explain how the distance between casinos affects their operations.
5. Discuss how a casino fits into its market affects its operations.
6. Discuss the importance of different modes of transportation to a casino's operations.
7. Detail the history of water, ground, and air transportation to a casino's operation.
8. Describe the importance of location and transportation in casinos.
9. Describe the importance of the originating state of visitors to casinos.
10. Explain the importance of the participation region of visitors to casinos.
11. Discuss the impacts of transportation on casino operations.

Endnotes

1. A portion of this chapter first appeared in Lee, C. (2008). Place. In Hashimoto, K. (2008). *Casino Management: A Strategic Approach*. Columbus, OH: Prentice Hall Publishing.

2. Plume, J. (2002). Any number can play. *Casino Journal*, 15(3), 32–37.

3. Bulavsky, J. (2002). The marketing manifesto. *Casino Journal*, 15(9), 75–77.

4. AGA State of the States (2008). Retrieved June 15, 2008, from http://www.americangaming.org/assets/file/aga_2008_sos.pdf.

5. Bulavsky, J. (2002). The marketing manifesto. *Casino Journal*, 15(9), 75–77.

6. Retrieved June 15, 2008, from http://philadelphia.areaconnect.com/statistics.htm; http://quickfacts.census.gov/qfd/states/36000.html; http://quickfacts.census.gov/qfd/states/09000.html.

7. Lee, C. (2008). Place. In Hashimoto, K. (2008). *Casino Management: A Strategic Approach.* Columbus, OH: Prentice Hall Publishing.

8. Harrah's Survey (2006). Retrieved June 18, 2008, from http://www.harrahs.com/images/PDFs/Profile_Survey_2006.pdf.

9. Lee, C. (2008). Place. In Hashimoto, K. (2008). *Casino Management: A Strategic Approach.* Columbus, OH: Prentice Hall Publishing.

10. AGA State of the States (2008). Retrieved June 15, 2008, from http://www.americangaming.org/assets/file/aga_2008_sos.pdf.

11. Morrison, A. M., Braunlich, C. G., Liping, A. C., and O'Leary, J. T. (1996). A profile of the casino resort vacationer. *Journal of Travel Research*, 35(Fall), 55–61.

CHAPTER 10

PROMOTIONS

KATHRYN HASHIMOTO

Learning Objectives

1. To introduce the reader to the four major promotional techniques[1]
2. To help the reader understand integrated marketing communications
3. To explain the difference between "push" and "pull" strategies
4. To provide the reader with an understanding of personal sales, sales promotion, public relations, and advertising
5. To introduce the several aspects that need to be considered when creating advertisements
6. To help the reader understand how direct marketing fits with the effective options casinos use to reach their customers

Chapter Outline

Introduction

Personal Sales

Sales Promotion

Public Relations or Publicity

Advertising

Direct Marketing

Conclusion

INTRODUCTION

Promotions are the links that a casino uses to communicate with the outside world. They can be personal interactions or group techniques designed to communicate a message to a large audience. As a rule there are four major promotional techniques: personal sales, sales promotion, public relations or publicity, and advertising. The best campaigns integrate and coordinate each of these communication channels so that there is one clear consistent message about the organization and its products. This is referred to as **IMC** (integrated marketing communications). This can result in a **synergistic strategy** in that the sum of the parts is greater than the whole.

In the IMC strategy, there are several factors that determine which of these promotional elements to use and when.

- First, the nature of the offering is important. A complimentary dinner for two at the restaurant is not appropriate for a mass audience message, but a personal invitation by a casino host or a direct mail piece would be.
- Second, there is a question of what type of strategy should be used: "push" or "pull." A **push strategy** tries to push the offer or package through the player's club or casino host to a player. This means that the casino wants its employees to make the offer and sell its product. On the other hand, in a **pull strategy**, the players learn of an offer and they then go to the casino to obtain the deal. The players are the ones who pull the offer from the casino.
- Third, it is important to understand where in the **buyer readiness stage** the potential client is. Are they new to casinos? Are they new to your particular casino? Are they new to the player's club? Are they new to casino hosts? Or, are they an old hand at the casino? In each of these cases, a different strategy and offer should be made.

For example, if you are looking for someone new to casinos, you might want to have a friend extend an invitation to spend some time at the casino. In this push strategy, an offer can be made to a regular player to invite ten of his/her best friends to a party at the casino. These friends are asked to fill out a player's club card while they are at the casino. This pushes the offer through the casino and obtains new players who might be interested in gambling now that they have been exposed to the casino. This strategy obtains new customers who are influenced by their friend who does the selling. On the other hand, a pull strategy would send out "comped" pairs of tickets to a concert in order to have the clients come to the casino and ask for their tickets. The clients are the ones who make the move toward the casino. Since it is hard to identify new gamblers, this offer might be better as a follow-up offer to the invitees from the previous party. They have been to the casino and gambled a little, and now the pull strategy encourages them to return again.

PERSONAL SALES

Personal sales are most effective with a well-trained staff, but it is the most expensive and labor-intensive process as well. This is a one-on-one interaction where one trained salesperson communicates with a single client. This technique requires a person who knows the product and is sensitive to the buyer's needs and can judge nuances in body language to create the most effective timing and exchange. To some degree, a superb salesperson is born; he/she instinctively knows the right thing to say at the right time, and he/she can automatically sense a client's moods.

Personal sales are frequently used in the casino environment. It used to be that the dealers were expected to "dummy up and deal" for security reasons. However, now dealers can have conversations with guests at the table. A likeable or lucky dealer can draw a gambler back to the casino. In addition, pit bosses and floor people also spend time getting to know their clientele. For example, a regular blackjack player, Don, goes back to the same casino because he likes the dealers and supervisors. When he walks in, everyone says "Hi Don!" He plays strictly by the same rules, and dealers who know his habits often can anticipate his actions. Don prides himself on the fact that the dealers know him and can almost play his hands for him, and sometimes do because he is so predictable. So, getting to know the customer personally can be a very effective sales tool.

Casino hosts are employees who are hired to anticipate and expedite a high roller's needs. Typically, they organize special, individual comps. Sometimes they can make the first move in a push strategy by inviting a high roller to celebrate an event like a birthday or an anniversary at the casino. At other times, a high roller may call the host and request that a party be arranged in a pull strategy. Hosts arrange suites and/or reservations for dining. They can make sure a favorite wine or food is readily available in the room. For example, in Atlantic City, there was a high roller who was so captivated by the *Batman* film that he demanded that the hotel recreate the bat cave for his room. Because he was such a

FIGURE 10.1 Getting to know the customer personally can be a very effective sales tool.

Source: Dorling Kindersley.

good customer with an extremely high credit limit, the hotel complied. Some casino hosts become so close to the high rollers that they become very good friends and are invited on trips unrelated to the casino property.

In contrast to personal sales, the other three promotional techniques communicate to large numbers of people at the same time.

SALES PROMOTION

The **sales promotion** is a reminder that is designed to quickly get the casino's name out to groups of people. This short-term strategy can draw traffic into the casino for a specified period of time, and it reminds people about the casino. There are several objectives for a promotion. Some promotions, such as drink, entertainment, or food discounts, are used to create immediate foot traffic in the casino. Once the people are in the casino, other promotions such as hourly drawings and double jackpot payoffs are designed to get them to stay longer. To get patrons to play table games, promotions can include bonus pay on certain blackjack hands or coupons that can be used in place of cash on table bets. To get customers to play the machines, free pulls or prizes tend to dominate the market.

A classic example of a sales promotion is the bus programs that were created by Atlantic City to encourage the millions of potential guests along the densely populated northeast corridor to take a chance. The programs were designed to be very affordable to help people get to the casino without driving a long distance. They were designed as social events with food, beverages, and entertainment to keep the people happy. When they got off the bus, they typically got a comped buffet and some tokens. When they got tired, and it was time to get on the bus, they slept the rest of the way home. In the beginning, the casinos gave $20 in tokens to each bus passenger. As a rule, the patrons spent the $20 plus another $60 of their own money. This made the bus promotion worthwhile for the casino. However, as competition for bus passengers increased, the offers became more expensive and some casinos almost went bankrupt because they spent more than they earned. The bus programs were done so often and so successfully that some casino marketers forgot that there is a limit to the amount of money the people spend. Early in Atlantic City's history, it is rumored that a casino went under because the marketers forgot that regular profitability checks are necessary for any offer.

Another sales promotion is the tournament. A tournament can introduce inexperienced gamblers to the fun and excitement of the games, and give them the opportunity to meet new people. A tournament generates additional gaming revenue and creates positive publicity for the casino. Finally, it expands the number of new members in the database.

According to a story, in 1961, a casino stockholder flew some wealthy friends from Florida to Las Vegas and the casino hotel paid for everything. While they stayed at the hotel, the casino recorded its biggest "drop" during their gambling spree. As a result, the casino began to experiment with this type of promotion, now called a "**junket**." By 1970 most Las Vegas Strip hotels had adopted junkets as a viable form of sales promotion. Junkets are completely comped, invited trips that are linked to special events such as boxing matches, PGA golf tournaments, or other highly sought-after events. While everything is paid for by the casino, it is expected that the gamblers will in turn spend equal amounts of time in the casino gambling.

PUBLIC RELATIONS OR PUBLICITY

Public relations is a promotional technique that attempts to inform people without controlling the message or media. This can be a press release announcing new games, jackpot winners, or changes in leadership, anything that goes through the media. Although the message is given to the media, the press can write anything they want about the event, or nothing at all. For example, an announcement of a new poker room can be written as a front-page story for a local casino newspaper, a page 10 story in a daily newspaper, or not at all for radio or television. Some announcements are simply faxes sent to media; others are announced at a press conference; and still others are accentuated with food, drink, and important dignitaries present.

FIGURE 10.2 Characters on trade show floors help attract customers to a booth.

For example, Las Vegas started a special publicity campaign in 1946. It was labeled "Hometown Art." The town publicist directed photographers to take pictures of attractive couples and families visiting the various resorts, especially when they were outdoors enjoying the sun and recreational activities. These photographs, along with short stories about the tourists and Las Vegas, were sent to the society editors of the tourists' hometown newspapers. This gave Las Vegas a positive reception in the local newspapers and created a more personal image. In another interesting publicity effort, in the 1950s and 1960s the Sahara created a professional journal for American barbers that was placed in barbershop magazine racks throughout the country. Along the same lines, the Sahara also created a national magazine for bellhops, which featured the winner of the magazine's bellman of the year contest. The Sahara estimated that 20% of the new customers who registered at the hotel were referred by bellhops in other cities.

ADVERTISING

Advertising is a controlled process. The casino creates the message and expects the media to communicate it exactly. The casino also pays for the timing and placement of the message. In this way, the public sees, hears, feels, touches, and smells exactly what the casino wants them to.

When creating advertisements, there are several aspects to consider. One of the common acronyms is **AIDA**—attention, interest, desire, action. An advertisement should gain a client's attention so that it can pique interest in the product. If you have targeted the audience correctly, once a person knows about the product, it should create a desire in the person to take an action. For example, an action can be to pick up the phone and call, or it can be to buy the product. Once you have gained a person's attention, the best way to give him/her the information is to "**KISS**" (keep it simple, stupid). Typically, you have about five seconds before the person moves on through the newspaper or magazine. In that time,

FIGURE 10.3 The first step of AIDA is attention. This billboard does an admirable job of getting the attention of every man driving by.

Source: Bill Aron/PhotoEdit Inc.

you have to let him/her know what your product is and why he/she should buy it. Therefore, making the message as simple as possible is important to getting the message across.

There are three major objectives to choose from with an advertisement. Do you want to inform, persuade, or remind? That is, do you want to tell people about a new offer or product? Or do they already know about the casino, so you now want to persuade them to come again or come more often? Or do you want to remind them that the casino is still in the same location and they should come for a visit because they haven't come for a while?

The final decision is to decide which media to use for the advertisement. Part of this decision is to understand reach and frequency. *Reach* refers to how many people actually use the media. For example, how many people listen to WWOZ radio at 8:00 A.M. on their way to work, or watch Channel 2 on television on Tuesday at 6:00 A.M.? In addition, *frequency* refers to how often people do something. For example, one of the positive aspects of a billboard is that people probably drive past the same billboard every day to work or school. In the 1960s and 1970s, northern Nevada casinos depended primarily on automobile traffic. Therefore, Harrah's created a highly successful billboard campaign by buying highway billboard space in a 500-mile radius leading into Reno and Lake Tahoe. As a rule, people need about five to six exposures before they truly begin to be aware of an ad. Therefore, a billboard is an attractive option because it has great frequency and repetition. Selecting the target audience and determining what they are doing at a particular time of day can also determine what media will be most successful in getting the message out.

However, developing advertisements is a relatively new issue for the gaming industry. On June 25, 1948, the federal government enacted 18 USC 1304 that strictly forbade any radio or television station from broadcasting any information concerning gambling or gaming. Therefore, casinos could advertise their food or hotels, but there could be no mention of people playing cards, dice, or slot machines. In fact, in 1984, the Casino Control Commission added additional constraints that made the federal laws even stronger. Product offerings had to be generic in nature, which made competing against another casino virtually impossible. Therefore, the advertising strategies kept the tone and style of the advertisements geared toward entertainment. Casino advertisements were filled with elegant men, pretty women in scant outfits, lots of lights, and lots of glamour. Finally, in 1999, the Greater New Orleans Broadcasting Association, Inc., challenged the ruling, and on June 14, 1999, the regulation was declared unconstitutional. Now casinos can show their true creativity by developing advertising campaigns like any other business.

DIRECT MARKETING

The traditional four types of promotions have begun to merge. Combinations of these promotions offer better, more effective options to reach the customers. Direct marketing is one of those options. **Direct marketing** develops interactive communication with the casino's best customers. It begins by building and maintaining a collection of personal information about players who enter the casino, as well as potential players. Direct response advertising asks a reader, viewer, or listener to provide feedback directly to the casino. For example, a casino might immediately send a new player a guest satisfaction survey when he/she returns home. In this fashion, the casino can discern a player's likes and dislikes about the casino experience. It is then possible to change the negative aspects of the casino and enhance the positive ones. Furthermore, offering a free gift or a chance to win a lottery for returning the survey enhances the chance for additional encounters with the gambler, as well as for obtaining valuable information. Sometimes, telemarketing can be used to sell or prospect a potential guest by telephone, to answer specific phone inquiries, or to provide sales-related services. If a guest has requested information, a telephone call is a nice personal touch. However, many people feel trapped by sales calls on the phone, especially when they disrupt meals or quiet times.

Direct mail involves sending an inexpensive bulk mailing to a target audience and possibly increases traffic in the casino. There are three elements to a direct mail campaign: the database, the offer, and the packaging. It has been suggested that 60% of the success of a direct mail piece is the quality of the database and the selection of criteria to target the appropriate audience. Obviously the offer is important, but it needs to be matched to the specific interests of the targeted person. For example, if I am a vegetarian, I am not going to be interested in a dinner for two at the steakhouse. Finally, it may be surprising to learn that the packaging or the appearance of the mailer is important. How do you pique someone's curiosity enough to even open the envelope and to read the offer rather than immediately throw everything in the trash can?

Some pointers that have worked are:

- Pretest the offer using a sample clientele from the database paired with a particular package before sending it to everyone. Using a small sample first allows you to see whether the offer is interesting before wasting money on a full-blown campaign.
- AIDA. Remember the acronym from earlier? First you need to attract people's attention so that you can gain their interest and fan their desire and so they will take action.
  - Gain their attention by asking a provocative question.
  - Keep their interest by using letters to create the personal touch. Letters seem to be more effective than postcards.
  - Keep the rules of etiquette by using words like *please* and *thank you*.
  - Use phrases such as "there is no obligation" or "no salesperson will call." They are stress relievers.
  - Stress the benefits of the offer, not the features. What will it do for them? This will fan their desire.
  - Close the sale with a "limited time" or a deadline. People tend to procrastinate. Even if it is a good offer and they like it, the envelope might sit on their desk for "when they get to it." Time limits create a sense of urgency to take action.

Direct marketing campaigns rely on using a very good database and segmenting the population of gamblers into smaller units that have some aspects in common. These commonalities could be something simple like having the same birthday or anniversary. However, it is very easy to get lazy and do the same thing for everyone. All casinos offer free food and hotel rooms. An overheard conversation might point out the problems. Two couples were sitting at a table in the casino; obviously they had just driven over together. "What offers do you have?" says Joe. "I have a free room at Casino A but it's not a suite so we all can't stay for free," says Sally. "That's okay," replies Tony, "I have an offer for a suite at Casino B." "Ok. So it's settled where to stay. Now where can we eat?" Offers are easily duplicated by competitors, so players can be inundated with a number of offers. In this case, casinos have trained the player's club members to be careful shoppers. They have learned that by pooling their resources, they can stay, eat, and be entertained for almost nothing. However, what is the point of the player's club? To build brand loyalty, but here it is clear that the exact opposite has occurred. Casinos have trained the players to go for the best offer rather than to be loyal to the brand.

FIGURE 10.4   Direct mail pieces can be personalized to target people better.

Personalizing the offer is critical, especially with gamblers who spend a lot of time and money at the casino. An old saying in research is, "If you want to know what your guests are thinking, ask them." Because these guests come often, an offer for another buffet may not be attractive. In fact, one regular customer said that the standard offers were offensive. In effect, he felt that the casino was sending a message that it did not care enough about him and his money to personalize the offer. He said that he knows all the dealers and floor people at the casino and talks to them on a regular basis. As a suggestion, why can't the floor person simply ask him what he wants?

Another regular guest on the Gulf Coast said he is not interested in the food or hotel offers; he lives a half hour away. So, when asked, "Is there something we can do for you?" he replied, "Yes. Occasionally I have some friends who want to get together, socialize, and gamble. So it would be great if on those occasions, I could call up my host and ask for comps for my friends." This gives casinos more guests in their database, more people gambling at their tables—sounds like a winner!

Conclusion

Communicating with guests takes a lot of research to learn who they are and what they like. There is no substitute for a good, well-maintained database. Always adding information to the database allows a manager to pick and choose what information is relevant for a particular offer. Combining personal information with a great promotion is always a winner. When the four types of promotions are integrated into one strategy, the effects can be spectacular. IMC is a way to think about the project as a whole, then to decide which promotion or combination of promotional ideas is the most effective.

Key Words

Advertising *131*
Promotions *127*
IMC *127*
Synergistic strategy *127*
Push strategies *127*
Pull strategies *127*

Buyer readiness stage *127*
Casino hosts *128*
Sales promotion *129*
Junket *129*
Public relations *130*
Advertising *130*

AIDA *131*
KISS *131*
Reach *132*
Frequency *132*
Direct marketing *132*

Review Questions

1. List the four major promotional techniques.
2. When using the IMC strategy, what are some factors that determine which promotional elements to use and when they should be used?
3. Which promotion is the most effective with a well-trained staff, but also the most expensive and labor intensive?   *Personal Sales*

4. What three promotional techniques communicate to large numbers of people at the same time?
5. What are the three major objectives to choose from with an advertisement?
6. In a direct mail piece, what methods can be used to pique someone's curiosity enough to open the envelope and to read the offer?

Endnote

1. A major portion of this chapter first appeared in Hashimoto, K. (2008). *Promotions in Casino* *Management: A Strategic Approach*. Columbus, OH: Prentice Hall Publishing.

CHAPTER 11

TYING IT ALL TOGETHER

Kathryn Hashimoto

Learning Objectives

1. To provide an understanding of the importance of strategic planning to casino marketing
2. To detail the importance of external environments to casino marketing
3. To detail how the nature of consumers and organizational buyers affect casino marketing
4. To learn how the details and qualities of the product of casinos (the games) affect casino marketing
5. To learn the importance of the service-profit chain to casino marketing
6. To create awareness of revenue management
7. To learn the importance of the various components of place to casino marketing
8. To understand the importance of the various components of promotions to casino marketing

Chapter Outline

INTRODUCTION

Often people think that marketing is just sales because those are the jobs that are readily available and most visible. However, the definition "finding a need and filling it" encompasses so much more. If you think from a strategic perspective, there are so many factors to having a successful business that it is easy to get lost in the day-to-day operations. That's why managers need to set aside specific times to meet and discuss "who are we, where are we going, and how do we plan to get there?" When wonderful new opportunities arise, some might want to take the chance and go for it.

However, understanding who you are allows you to step back and assess whether the current strengths and weaknesses of the corporation are aligned with the new challenge. In some cases, knowing the history of the company allows people to say, "Yes that is a great opportunity for someone, but not us. We have already been down that road before you came to the company and it did not work." In other cases, in assessing a new project, there would be too many changes and too many new skills that would be needed to implement it. Therefore, the company is not ready yet to go in this direction. However, with planning, the company could be ready sometime down the road. As a result, objectives are set and detailed plans are laid out for time frames and goals to be met.

STRATEGIC PLANNING

At **G2E** (Global Gaming Expo, the largest global gaming trade show and exposition) one year, a speaker was talking about strategic planning. A person raised his hand from the crowd and said, "Strategic planning doesn't work. We have tried it. We assessed where we were and agreed on the new direction. But we never reached our goals; so what good was all that work?" As the man in the crowd continued to talk, it was clear that his casino managers had done the first two steps, but had not completed the third, longest, and most important step—planning.

There are three main parts to planning. First, there is the setting of objectives and breaking each one down into doable, quantifiable goals. Quantifiable is one of the key parts. It means being able to attach a specific measure to an objective, for example, "We want to increase sales by 10% by next July." Everyone can understand 10% and what it means for them. Then you must divide that task into more specific quantifiable measures, such as "The sales force needs to focus some of their attention on filling the gap in next February's calendar with two groups of 5,000 or more attendees which should generate $50,000 profit. All other things being equal, this should allow us to increase sales by 5%." As you can see, it will be easy for the sales manager to go back to his/her department, break these goals into smaller tasks, and begin allocating responsibility to each person who will complete each part. When each salesperson completes his/her part, the goals will be accomplished.

The second part of planning is time management. After all, if the goal must be reached by next February but Tom and Sally don't complete their tasks until next December, then we have a problem. Therefore, each task must also have a set date to completion. This allows us to stagger deadlines so that one task can be built on another task or multiple tasks can reach completion at the same time so that all the tasks can be compiled to build a total objective.

The third and last part of planning is assigning responsibility. Who will be responsible for each part? Who is in charge to make sure that everyone is on the same page? Who

FIGURE 11.1 This solitary empty booth on a very busy trade-show floor indicates that someone's plan did not work.

is in charge to make sure that everyone is progressing at a pace that will ensure that they will be done on time? Unfortunately, if we just say we have to do this project without anyone taking responsibility, the project will never happen. It is human nature to allow someone else to do a task if it is not our job. Therefore, make sure everyone understands what his/her job is, when it is due, and who will be overseeing the project, so that the pieces of the puzzle fall into place at the assigned time.

So, **strategic planning** is the overview of what should happen in the casino resort. However, in order for us to create a reasonable, successful plan, there are **macromarketing** factors that need to be understood and assessed in terms of their impact on the property—external factors that the casino resort cannot control but that will play a role in what happens. For example, is there an impact on a casino in Las Vegas if there is the snowstorm of the century in New Jersey? What would those effects be? Well, Newark Airport would probably be shut down for at least a day. This means that any airline flying in and out of New Jersey would be impacted. Planes would not arrive on time in most of the United States because each flight is based on changing planes at specific airports at designated times. The whole plan is disrupted because planes are not where they should be. Gamblers flying to Las Vegas may not be able to get there on Friday for their weekend stay because they are snowed in New Jersey or their flights are cancelled in Chicago. By the time the flights are straightened out and running, it may be Saturday, but the gambler has to work on Monday morning. Is it worth the trip for one day? Therefore, the casino in Las Vegas finds itself with many cancellations for the hotel which means there will be fewer people gambling, eating at the restaurants, or buying souvenirs and clothes at the shopping mall. Quickly, the situation must be assessed and new plans have to be made. A casino might lower prices for the weekend, hoping to attract drive-in traffic. The casino staff could call or e-mail to offer local clients a special last-minute promotion for the coming weekend.

EXTERNAL ENVIRONMENTS

So, it is important to be on top of what is happening around the world. Economic conditions or employment patterns may mean that people are afraid to travel or gamble because they are more concerned that they won't have jobs in the near future, so they save their money just in case. Or the reverse condition, where the economy is doing well and growing, people are confident and spending money on recreation and vacations. Now that gambling is considered to be both a recreation for locals and a vacation for tourists, it is part of the American cultural and social environment. This is a positive turn of events, after a history of negativism. However, the casinos need to be aware that if any of the negatives of gaming are not controlled, the political and legal environments can limit or even deregulate gaming. On the other hand, if governments like the tax dollars coming from gambling, they can ease the restrictions. In New Orleans, Harrah's threatened to pull out if concessions could not be made in terms of their tax rate and their ability to have a hotel and restaurants. Since the city and state were already dependent on the revenue from the gambling dollars, they agreed to make it easier for Harrah's to do business.

The macromarketing or **external environments** impact the competitive environment and also the buyer behaviors of clients. If the macromarketing environment is good for business, then more competitors will enter the field to take advantage of the opportunities. For example, we typically think of casino properties needing hotels and restaurants. However, there are a number of hotel chains that decided to take advantage of their location by adding a casino to their properties because of the lucrative profit margins. Hotels already attract a certain clientele, so if they understand their guests' buying behaviors, adding a casino might enhance their attractiveness and draw even more people to the property.

CONSUMERS AND ORGANIZATIONAL BUYERS

As we saw, there are two major types of clients, consumers and organizational buyers. Consumers are individuals who purchase the product for themselves or who decide to go gambling. There are many reasons why people gamble: to have an adrenaline rush, to make money, to have fun, or to join their friends. Gamblers come from all walks of life, all income levels, and all lifestyles. There are no demographic parameters that can predict who will enjoy gambling. However, we can use demographic profiles to decide whom to attract, seniors, "20- to 30-somethings," or people with incomes over $100,000. As we research these people who fit our profile, we look for psychographics like activities, interests, and opinions to find common motivations to come to our casino. Seniors might be housebound and looking for some adventure or just some time walking on the beach. Twenty- to thirty-somethings may be driven to be with friends and party. People with incomes over $100,000 may also be social but they want to do it in style, with champagne and caviar, instead of beer and chips.

We can also examine the geographic location our guests come from so that we can make our media selection easier and more productive. Sometimes we look at what they do and how often they make the decision to gamble or travel to gaming destinations. Since they already like to go to casinos, we might want to see if they can come more often or stay longer. In addition, all the members of these groups may have friends who are like them, so they could be potential loyal customers. All we need to do is get them to the casino and

FIGURE 11.2 Attendees at conferences are less price sensitive in terms of their room rates and food.

hope the casino environment and staff will do the rest. So, we invite friends and families to a special party just for them. We give them a little status, a little recognition, and a little player's club card to help them get started.

Organizational consumers are a little different. Because you are dealing with a group of people, you need to identify the decision maker as well as the influential people in the group. Understanding how the meeting planners fit into the equation and who makes the final decision on destination is important. The meeting planner can be a long-term role because he/she can influence many different groups' decisions to come to the casino resort. Therefore, understanding how groups think and what they are looking for in a destination makes it easier to sell the property and its amenities. Usually the meeting planner and group planner are on the same wavelength. They want the same things. However, that is not always the case. As a result, it is important to meet the group planners to identify their needs and desires. Large groups may only have a convention once a year but they may bring more attendees. On the other hand, a corporate meeting planner may not have a large group, but they may come to the resort more often, bringing many different constituents from the same corporation. Casinos have not always embraced group business, but with the new revenue-management software, they can sort out which groups are good for business and which groups have minimal profit margins. Therefore, it is easier to segment both consumer and organizational buyers now that the casino can analyze each person or group's profitability to offer the best rates and availability.

Therefore, the casinos are focusing on **micromarketing** (things they can control) factors like product, price, place, and promotion as a way to plan around threats and to enhance the opportunities that come their way. In addition, as the weaknesses in the product are assessed, plans to turn these weaknesses into strengths should also be onboard. For example, one of the consistent problems in the social environment of gaming has always been gaming addiction. Casinos have worked with Gamblers Anonymous to see how they could be involved and minimize the problems. Then, over the last few years managers have begun to realize that now that they understand the issues, they can create their own programs with responsible gaming.

THE PRODUCT—GAMES

Of course, the games are always the top attraction for tourists, but the reality is that everyone has table games and slots. They might have different product assortments but essentially they all work the same. Therefore, in many consumers' perceptions, a casino is a casino is a casino. However, there is one product that casinos cannot copy from each other—the individual employee. Gamblers might be attracted to a dealer or pit boss because of superstition or simply because they like the person. It gives a person a warm, fuzzy feeling to walk into the casino and have employees call you by your first name and ask how your day is going. It gives your ego a boost to know that you are important enough for people to bother to learn your name. After all, in some regular jobs, you don't get that kind of respect. Therefore, the casino works to make you feel like a VIP.

This is pretty heady stuff. More importantly, the **service-profit chain** theory created at Harvard Business School actually works! If you treat your employees right, they will be content in their jobs. This results in less turnover, and less hiring and training expenses for the casino. In addition, happy employees will pass this job satisfaction on to their guests. When the guests are happy, they want to come more often and tend to be more loyal to the casino. This results in better guest relations, which translates into more profitability for the company. Not only has this been shown to make more money, but it even shows up in the stock prices of publicly held casinos.

SERVICE-PROFIT CHAIN

Gary Loveman, now CEO and president of Harrah's, was one of the original authors of that seminal article on the service-profit chain. Because of that article, in 1998, he was hired to show everyone how it worked in the real world. There are media stories that claim Gary Loveman jokes about when he first joined the management team at Harrah's. "They hired a professor and expected me to last a week, but I surprised them." So the story goes. His efforts to show the viability of his theory worked at Harrah's. Profits soared under his leadership. Five years after he was hired, these were some of the headlines from the national newswire services in 2003:

> Harrah's Entertainment Captures National Information Technology Award
> Harrah's Entertainment Captures 564 Awards in Strictly Slots Readers' Poll
> Harrah's Total Rewards Earns Web Smart 50 Honor from BusinessWeek
> Harrah's Entertainment Honored with National Social Responsibility Award
> Harrah's Wins Top Quarterly Hospitality Ranking in Casino Industry from
>   Market Matrix Survey of 35,000 Consumers

FIGURE 11.3   Rio is now part of the Harrah's Entertainment.

Harrah's Entertainment Named to Dow Jones Sustainability World Index for
    Third Consecutive Year
Harrah's Entertainment Board of Directors Named Best in Gaming Industry
Harrah's Entertainment Captures Top 10 Spot for Fifth Straight Year in
    Computerworld's "Best Places to Work in Information Technology" Ranking
Harrah's Entertainment Top-Ranked Gaming Company in Barron's 500
Harrah's Entertainment Named Top Casino Hotel Brand in Customer
    Satisfaction Survey
Harrah's Entertainment Honored with Restaurant Industry "Employer of
    Choice" Award

The service-profit chain theory worked in practice.

REVENUE MANAGEMENT

In the other books in this gaming series, we discuss pricing from a number of perspectives. We discuss the concept of house advantage and game rules to name a few perspectives. So in this book, we explored the relatively new pricing strategy of using computer software called **Revenue Management**. In casinos, revenue-management software basically takes all the variables on a guest's spending habits and creates a profile that can be used to calculate a gambler's worth. From this standpoint, the computer makes a recommendation on room rate and comp status. Of course, software is only as good as the inputs it receives. Therefore, a person always looks at the information to decide whether it should stand or if there is additional information that is not in the computer that will change a person's status.

PLACE

Once we determine product and price, place is the third micromarketing variable. Place includes both channels of distribution, as well as physical distribution. The channels of distribution are the different businesses that are used between the guest and the casino. Travel agents and tour operators are some of the intermediaries who might help us bring tourists to the casino. However, location is one of the variables that makes it easy or difficult to promote the casino. If you have a casino that is in the midst of a group of attractions like New Orleans where people come for the festivals, food, and good times, then it is relatively easy to draw tourists to the casino. On the other hand, if the casino is located in a remote location far away from other tourist attractions, then it is more important to be able to draw locals. The site of the casino then is an important determinant for our strategic plan. The other aspect of place is the physical distribution or transportation. How do people arrive at the casino? How easy is it? Many destinations like Las Vegas and Atlantic City created large airports to be able to fly guests in from anywhere in the world. Other local casinos plan on their guests arriving by car from their nearby homes. So, channels, location, and transportation are very important factors when assessing our strengths and weaknesses and planning for the future.

PROMOTIONS

Finally, **promotions** take everything about casinos and creates messages to show the public who we are and why they want to come. For a number of years, casinos were not allowed to advertise gambling except in very generic fun scenarios. However, once the courts ruled that casinos should be able to advertise and create promotions that show their

FIGURE 11.4 Having a casino on the Carnival Conquest ship makes it easier to find a great location.

product in action, marketers have been able to create more effective campaigns. However, the strongest promotions for the casinos have been in the area of direct marketing. Since casinos were not able to advertise for many years, they spent time and money to find out as much as possible about their guests. Then, armed with this information, they created mailers, cards, and promotions that selected specific target audiences and offered them special events that were designed to motivate them. Unlike other promotions that were designed to tap a broad audience, the direct marketing pieces could be tailored for a very small audience and hit all the motivational buttons.

Conclusion

So, tying it all together, marketing is more than just sales or advertising. It includes the total experience of analyzing the external conditions that impact the competitive environment and the buying public. Understanding how these changing conditions impact the guest is crucial to creating a more productive product. This environmental scanning allows casinos to predict how gamblers will respond to the uncontrollable variables so that they can create a plan on how to circumvent problems and create opportunities using the variables of product, price, place, and promotion. Once the manager understands what the client wants and needs, then decisions about the four p's of marketing is facilitated.

Key Words

G2E *137*

Strategic planning *138*

Macromarketing *138*

External environments *139*

Organizational consumers *140*

Micromarketing *140*

Service-profit chain *141*

Revenue management *142*

Promotions *143*

Review Questions

1. Explain the importance of strategic planning to casino marketing.
2. Detail the importance of external environments to casino marketing.
3. Detail how the nature of consumers and organizational buyers affect casino marketing.
4. Explain how the details and qualities of the product of casinos (the games) affect casino marketing.
5. Detail the importance of the service-profit chain to casino marketing.
6. Discuss the importance of the various components of place to casino marketing.
7. Discuss the importance of the various components of promotions to casino marketing.

CONTRIBUTOR'S BIOGRAPHIES

Christopher M. Hurley is a graduate student at East Carolina University studying to obtain his MBA in hospitality management. Christopher was born and grew up in Cleveland, Ohio, before moving to North Carolina in 2004 to further his education. For the past year, Christopher has worked as a graduate assistant performing research and assisting with classes under two professors at the university. Christopher's recent studies have focused on the casino industry. As part of his training for writing the strategy chapter (Chapter 2), Christopher interviewed nine different managers from a variety of casinos and levels of responsibility.

George G. Fenich, PhD is a professor in the Department of Hospitality Management at East Carolina University. He was a practitioner in the hospitality industry for 15 years before joining academe in 1985. His Ph.D. from Rutgers University is in tourism planning and policy development. His dissertation was entitled "The Dollars and Sense of Convention Centers." In the mid-1980s he also began researching and writing about casinos, including a widely used text on the subject. He has published over 30 research articles and done over 75 seminars and presentations to both academe and industry. He also sits on the editorial board of six academic journals. He published a book on the meetings and conventions industry and was awarded PCMA (Professional Convention Management Association) Educator of the year.

David Williams has worked in the casino industry over the past 15 years both in the United States and overseas, with Native American, riverboat, and large destination market experience. His articles have been published in industry magazines such as *Casino Journal, Casino Executive,* and *Casino International.* He has held positions ranging from marketing analyst to chief operating officer. David holds a BS in mathematics, computer science, and psychology from Emory & Henry College and an MBA from Vanderbilt University, and is currently a doctoral candidate at the University of Phoenix.

Kathryn Hashimoto spent over 10 years in resort management before moving to university teaching in marketing, service, and hospitality. During this time, Dr. Hashimoto has published 6 books, written over 30 articles, and presented numerous times on casino management. Kathryn testified before the Public Gaming Sector Commission and the Rhode Island Finance Committee on the impact of casinos and was a column writer for Casino Enterprise Management. One of her proudest achievements was to work with the only aboriginal university in the world, First Nations University of Canada, to create their first program in hospitality and gaming. Currently, Dr. Hashimoto has a new casino management and a new introduction to hospitality textbook and now this Casino Essential Series.

INDEX